HOW TO CHOOSE AND ENJOY
W·I·N·E

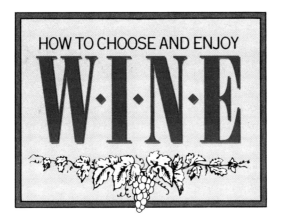

HOW TO CHOOSE AND ENJOY
W·I·N·E

JANCIS ROBINSON

Acknowledgements

The author and publishers would like to thank the following for the illustrations in this book. *Photographs* Archivio IGDA 89; Anthony Blake 48-9, 55 left, 70-71, 72, 98; Colman's of Norwich Wines 112; Colour Library International 109; Comité Interprofessionnel Des Vins de Bourgogne 63 right; Food & Wine from France 49, 83; Fotobank International Colour Library 58, 79 right; The Image Bank 61, 99; Picturepoint 84-5, 96, 101; Wine & Spirit Education Trust Limited 50, 63 left; Zefa 75, 77, 79 left, 93, 105; Tony Chau, front cover (inset); *Special Photography* James Jackson; *Maps* David Humphrys; *Cover Design* James Waugh of Snap Design. Thanks are also due to John Milroy Limited, O. W. Loeb & Company Limited and Barwell & Jones for their assistance with wine and wine labels.

This edition published exclusively for Ferroway Limited (Fanfare Books) in 1985 by Orbis Publishing Limited, London

ISBN 0-86370-002-0
Printed in Great Britain.

CONTENTS

INTRODUCTION

WINE IS FUN

Wine is, indisputably, fun. It is only our fears about the subject, invariably induced by someone else, that get in the way of what should be our unselfconscious and easy-going enjoyment of this wonderful liquid.

It is absurd that wine is regarded by many people as a complicated and slightly awesome subject. It is, after all, a basic agricultural commodity. Many Italians, for instance, still see water as a more suspect thirst-quencher than wine. For them, wine is something quite natural – like vegetables grown in the back garden. In France, most wine is still regarded as something as necessary as salt with meals, but not nearly grand enough to offer guests as an aperitif. Why is it, then, that so many people still feel wary?

The difference of course is that France and Italy are the world's major wine producers and a tax on wine drinking there would be both unpopular and commercially foolish. In this country, on the other hand, very few people have first-hand knowledge of wine production, but all wine drinkers have to pay heavily for their pleasure. Even the most mediocre wine costs about the same as 10 pints of milk once British excise duty has been paid on it. Undue reverence for something so relatively expensive is thus understandable.

It is useful to remember, however, when grappling with the complexities of a restaurant's wine list (which the wine-waiter probably understands little better than you) or scanning the shelves of the wine shop as you search for a ·

6

familiar name, that to most Europeans wine is a drink as simple as a cup of tea is to the British or coffee to Americans.

Admittedly, what makes wine such fun is also what starts to make it a little complicated: its enormous variety. Wine comes from all over the world, from a wide range of different vines planted in different soils, cultivated in different ways in varying weather conditions. Superimpose on all those natural variables the aims and methods of thousands of different winemakers around the world, and it seems hardly surprising that wine has such variety. But it is not, as the wine snob might like to suggest to the novice, an impenetrable jungle of names and jargon.

Wines are like any genetic group. There are family resemblances (between, say, the wines from the same vine type, wherever they are planted) and groupings that can be tasted (the light colour and high acidity of all wines made far from the equator, for example). It is building up your knowledge of the wine tribe's patterns and peculiarities that makes wine drinking such fun. All that is needed is an open mind, to take in as many of the clues as are offered, and a healthy disregard for anything that gets in the way of how you personally enjoy the contents of the glass in your hand.

Nowadays things are a little easier for those who want to learn about wine without necessarily learning about bankruptcy. An ever higher proportion of wine shops and wine businesses are staffed by genuinely knowledgeable and helpful people. Licensed supermarkets offer the chance to try out bottles at reasonable prices. Their wines are usually well-described on the label and shelf, and there are more and more straightforward books on the subject. Above all, I hope this one convinces you that wine is fun.

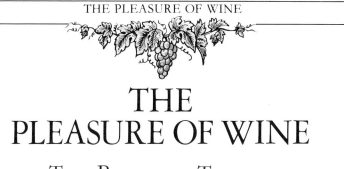

THE PLEASURE OF WINE

THE BASICS OF TASTING

'Tasting' sounds rather grand, but all it means is a rewarding blend of drinking and thinking. Every glass of wine we drink represents a whole year of vineyard cultivation and perhaps several years of effort in the winery. It costs considerably more than a newspaper, yet most of us throw it away, straight down our throats, without even trying to 'read' it.

Each wine has a story to tell and pleasure to give, but the simple way to benefit from the story and the pleasure remains unknown to most of those who spend their hard-earned cash on wine. The trick costs nothing, takes very little time, and has the great advantages of being neither fattening nor intoxicating. This is the secret – always sniff before you drink.

The sense of smell is much more refined and informative than any sensing equipment located in the mouth. If you are sceptical about this, think of the last time you had a cold. You didn't want to eat because your nose was blocked up and you had no sense of smell to stimulate your appetite. The food that you did eat tasted bland and boring, because all you had to rely on were the sensors inside your mouth.

Thousands of taste buds constitute the mouth's main sensing equipment, and in adults most of them are concentrated on the tongue. As a convenient shorthand, four basic tastes have been identified – sweetness, sourness, saltiness and bitterness – and different areas of the tongue are particularly sensitive to each. The tip of the tongue is especially good at picking up sweetness; the upper edges

9

sourness; the front edges saltiness; and the back flat part bitterness. This is only a model. Many people find that it is the underside of their tongue that is particularly sensitive to saltiness, for instance, and we all have slightly different sensitivities to different tastes.

This physiological theory holds as well for wine as for anything else tasted. Few wines are at all salty, however, and only a few Italian reds show much bitterness. Sweetness and sourness, or acidity, play the crucial roles in wines. All wines are fairly high in acid. Acidity is tartness when in excess, and called 'crispness' when there's just enough to enliven. This is what makes wine, and most other beverages, refreshing.

As a grape ripens, its acid level falls and its sugar level rises. It is only because ripe grapes contain fermentable sugar that we have wine at all. All or part of the grape's sugar is converted into alcohol during fermentation leaving a wine that is, respectively, either strong and dry or less strong and still retaining some unfermented sugar. The amount of acid in any wine reflects how ripe the grapes were when picked. The lower the acid, the more completely the grapes were ripened.

Wines made in hot climates, such as North Africa or the eastern Mediterranean, are noticeably low in acid and high in sugar or alcohol. The only ways a winemaker in a hot region can compensate for this is either by picking the grapes early, before they are fully ripe, or by carefully adding acid to the wine.

Wines made far from the equator, such as the Muscadet of France or English wines, are marked by high acidity and fairly low sugar or alcohol. French winemakers in the cooler regions compensate for this by adding sugar before fermentation to make the resultant wine stronger (but not sweeter). This common practice is called chaptalization. German winemakers have a completely different view and often add some unfermented sweet grape juice to make their wines sweeter, and less alcoholic, than they might be otherwise.

Every bottle of wine has its own complex story to tell.

Provided the whole tongue is exposed to a wine, by taking a nice big mouthful, the mouth can send messages to the brain about how sweet and how acid the wine is, but that is just about all. The really interesting part of a wine, its flavour, will elude the taste buds. A more sensitive piece of equipment is needed – the nose.

NOSING

We may think that we drink liquids and eat solids, but in fact we digest liquids and taste gases. It is only the action of saliva on solid foods that makes them digestible by turning them into liquids – and all we can do to 'taste' those liquids is to monitor them for the basics such as sweetness and acidity on our tongues.

To get to grips with the flavour of anything, we have to use our hypersensitive, and rather nasty sounding, olfactory

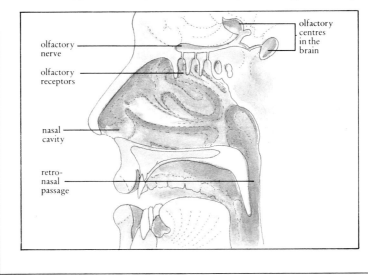

olfactory centres in the brain

olfactory nerve

olfactory receptors

nasal cavity

retro-nasal passage

Assessing a wine: first examine the colour, depth of colour and clarity of a wine by tilting the glass away from you against a light background (above left); second, gently swirl the wine around (above); third, smell (or 'nose') the wine by taking a short, concentrated sniff with your mouth slightly open (left). Opposite *The routes taken by the vapour when you smell wine.*

receptors which are located at the top of the nose. These react not to liquid but to the gas or vapour that any substance gives off, and send complex messages about the make-up of that vapour to the brain. The vapour is made up of all the tiny volatile elements that spring up into the atmosphere from the surface of a substance and is known as its 'smell'. Some

substances give off more smell than others. Glass is not smelly at all (which is why it is such a good material from which to taste wine), while flowers, for instance, are very volatile and give off lots of vapour into the atmosphere.

Wine and most foods are very volatile, with lots of vapour sending intricate messages to the brain via the olfactory receptors. As we have seen, the mouth can only relay much cruder messages than these. In fact what we think of as a food's or drink's 'smell' is actually what most of us call its 'taste'. 'Flavour' is perhaps a less confusing word for the mix of tiny volatile elements that go to make up each wine's individual character.

The vapour can reach the olfactory receptors by two possible routes: either straight up the nose or from the back of the mouth up what is known as the 'retro-nasal passage'. This is why even if you have never consciously sniffed a glass of wine, you will have had some inkling of the different flavours. Some of the vapour will naturally rise up the retro-nasal passage from each mouthful. Far more efficient as a way of enjoying the flavour of a wine, however, is to make sure your nose has a good sniff of it before taking any of it in your mouth.

All of this takes a fair time to explain, but takes no time at all to put into practice. To maximize the amount of vapour released by the wine, it is a good idea to maximize the surface area of it in contact with air. You can do this by gently swirling the wine around in the glass before taking a short, concentrated sniff just over the glass. There is no need for a very deep breath. All that is needed is to channel the vapour given off up the nose to the olfactory receptors, not to suck it down into the lungs. A moment's concentration on what messages this vapour has sent to the brain will be rewarded with one of the greatest pleasures that wine is capable of giving.

THE LOOK OF A WINE

Even before the nose has gone into action, and perhaps long before the mouth is exposed to a wine, the eyes can give quite a lot of information about it.

Every wine should be clear and bright. If a wine is murky then it may well be suffering from some fault, such as taint from an unclean container. If it has lots of tiny particles suspended in it and is a fairly old vintage, then perhaps all this means is that it should have been decanted off this sediment. On page 18 are details of how to do this. Before decanting, the bottle should be left to stand, still stoppered up for at least two days to allow the sediment time to settle to the bottom. Don't worry if a wine has little bits of cork floating in it. This will probably be the fault of the person who opened the bottle rather than its contents. Simply pick the bits out and enjoy the wine.

If a white wine has white crystals in it, there is usually a surprisingly comforting explanation. Tartaric acid is one of the acids commonly found in wine, and it can easily be crystallized by a sudden drop in temperature. If a wine has been kept somewhere very cold, therefore, 'tartrates' may form, and taste no more harmful than their first cousin, cream of tartar. Depending on how a bottle has been stored, these crystals may be found on the cork instead of floating in the wine and are equally harmless. In red wines, such crystals are dyed black, and may form part of the sediment.

A slight sparkle in a wine may be there with the intention of giving it a bit of pep (this is very common in Australian whites, young Chianti and Vinho Verde for instance) but it just may signal that something is wrong and a second fermentation has started in the bottle. If this is the case the wine will usually be cloudy.

The colour of a wine is a good clue to its age and,

sometimes, provenance. All wines go browner with age, so a red wine starts life as a purplish red and turns brick-coloured, then tawny. White wines go slightly and then very tawny with the years. The difference is that regardless of the actual hue, red wines get paler with age, while whites get darker. A deep golden-brown wine will almost certainly be very mature, unless it has oxidized, i.e. been exposed to too much air and 'gone off' to staleness. A deep crimson wine, on the other hand, will probably be very youthful.

Colouring matter for wines comes from the grapeskins, so the depth of colour in a wine can indicate more than age. A very deep-red wine will probably have been made either

The Beaujolais (left) is purple and not very deep, respectively because it's young and made fast. The claret on the right is paler and browner than the one in the middle because it's older.

somewhere very dry where the grapeskins were very thick, or by leaving the wine in contact with the skins for a long time, as in Bordeaux, or from a grape variety whose skins are naturally very high in colouring matter, such as Nebbiolo and Syrah. If a red wine is particularly pale, then this probably means it was made far from the equator where the sun had to struggle to ripen the grapes as in the red wines of Germany, or in a particularly cool year such as 1977 Bordeaux. Paleness in a red wine may also indicate that it was made by fermenting very fast such as is the custom in Beaujolais, or from a grape variety, such as Pinot Noir, that is not usually high in colouring matter.

The two burgundies on the left show how older wines, such as the one in the middle, go deeper and eventually browner with age. The Muscadet on the right is almost colourless.

If a white wine has very little colour at all, then it was probably made somewhere very cool, and vice versa. A slight greenish tinge often indicates the northern limits of vine cultivation, such as Mosel in Germany or Muscadet.

The best way to judge the intensity of colour is to look straight down into a glass from above, preferably against a plain white surface, and see how easy it is to pick out the bottom of the glass through the wine. The best way of judging the hue is to tip the glass away from you, again against a light surface, and look at the colour near the rim.

How to Taste

We have seen that the nose is vital for enjoyment and that the eyes can be helpful if you are playing that near-useless but impressive party game of trying to identify a wine 'blind', that is without first knowing what it is. The mouth is of course essential for the monitoring of sweetness and acidity, and for the following further aspects of wine drinking.

TANNIN This is not a basic taste, but can only be sensed by the mouth. Tannin is extracted along with colouring matter from grapeskins and is good at preserving red wines until they are interesting and mature. It is most noticeable when the wine is very young, and then gradually fades to allow the natural fruit in a wine to show the way it has matured. There is a lot of tannin in tea, and a very tannic wine has the same effect on the mouth as stewed tea, drying out the gums and the inside of the cheeks.

LENGTH AND AFTERTASTE The length of time a wine lingers in the mouth after it has been swallowed is a very good indicator of its quality. The longer the wine seems to reverberate around the back of the mouth and throat, the better it is. Such wines are called 'long' and said to have a

'long finish' or 'long aftertaste'. If a wine leaves no aftertaste, it is said to be 'short' and reckoned to be of fairly basic quality. A glass of great wine should take much longer to drink than a poor one, so long should each mouthful last.

Tasting notes serve as a much more reliable reminder of good bottles drunk in the past than the memory.

ALCOHOL This is the component that makes wine so much more interesting than grape juice, and is also the one that tends to make wine gatherings such sociable affairs. When the wine is in the mouth it is possible, with practice, to judge how alcoholic or 'full-bodied' a wine is. Just as a mouthful of cream feels heavier in the mouth than water, so different wines have a 'weight'. The higher the alcohol content of a wine, the heavier it is and the more 'body' it is said to have. Very alcoholic wines, such as port or some California Chardonnays, leave such an alcoholic aftertaste that the taster feels that his breath should be kept well away from naked flames. There are more details about the alcohol content of different wines on page 41.

Professional tasters see alcohol as a necessary evil and try to stay as sober as possible while they taste up to 100 different wines at a single session. This is done by spitting out every mouthful into a special container, called a spittoon. This practice looks disgusting to outsiders, but seems perfectly natural – nay vital – within the confines of the tasting room. The wine taster has no excuse for drinking at all: the throat is devoid of useful sensory equipment and there is no need to swallow a wine in order to taste it.

To sum up:

STEP ONE Look at the wine by tilting it away from you to note its clarity and colour.

STEP TWO Swirl the wine around in the glass and take a short, sharp sniff, noting and savouring the nuances of flavour.

STEP THREE Take a good mouthful so that all of the tongue is covered and notice what happens to the tip of the tongue (for sweetness), the upper edges (for acidity) and the inside of the mouth (for tannin).

STEP FOUR While the wine is in the mouth, try to gauge its weight, and just after you have swallowed it (or spat it out!) notice how 'long' it is.

OPENING THE BOTTLE

There is a lot to be said for the screw cap, especially after we have struggled with the impenetrable capsule and crumbling cork that so often seem designed to separate us from the wine we want to drink. In fact, a simple screw cap would be perfectly adequate for the vast majority of wines: those that are designed to be drunk within a year or two of being bottled. There is even some Australian research that suggests the screw cap keeps wine just as well as a cork and capsule for much longer periods. However, it is thought by most bottlers that the pop of the cork represents an important part of our enjoyment of wine, and is something worth spending money on. So in most cases we are still saddled with the business of wrestling with capsules and corks.

A capsule (the foil covering the top and the neck of the bottle) is put on mainly for cosmetic reasons but partly to protect the cork from a very rare bug called a cork weevil. Plastic ones are the most difficult to remove and may call for a very sharp knife. Foil and thin metal capsules can usually be cut more simply with the tip of a corkscrew. To leave the bottle looking attractive, the capsule should be cut in a neat line round the bottle neck close to the rim. To ensure there is no possibility of contamination from the capsule, especially important if it is made of lead, this line should be at least $\frac{1}{4}$ in (6 mm) from the rim. If you remove the capsule altogether, the wine will of course taste exactly the same, but some people think that the bottle looks naked.

There is an enormous range of different instruments that can be called into play for removing the cork. The most efficient corkscrews do actually have a *screw* which is a spiral coil of metal as opposed to a rivet with a coil embossed on it. The gadget that pumps carbon dioxide into the bottle to force out the cork can go disastrously wrong and it has been known

for bottles with faults in the glass to explode.

If the cork breaks before all of it has been extracted, try to remove the remains with your corkscrew in the usual way. If this fails, push it in sharply – with the end of a wooden spoon for example – and pour the wine out carefully over it. The 'butler's friend', a two-pronged instrument for coaxing out old and potentially delicate corks, may also be useful in this situation.

GLASSES

Glass is the ideal material from which to drink wine, not just because it imparts no distracting flavour of its own (unlike pottery, for instance), but also because it shows off a wine's colour to advantage. For this latter reason, purists prefer plain, uncut, colourless glass, as thin as possible so as to get the senses, literally, as close as possible to what the wine has to offer.

The ideal wine glass has a stem. This is partly to make the all-important swirling easier, and partly to ensure that a wine best enjoyed cool is not warmed up by the drinker's hand. Wine also tends to look more appetizing if not in a container smeared with greasy fingers! In some circumstances, such as under a tree in the Provençal sunshine, it is certainly possible to enjoy a rough country wine in thick tumblers, just as in such a setting, ice cubes and red wine can seem an entirely suitable mixture. It is a waste of fine wine, however, to serve it in a glass without a stem – just as it would be a shame to dilute the concentration of a great claret with ice cubes.

The vapour given off by a wine is, as we have seen, its most important attribute. Swirling the wine about in the glass by the stem releases this vapour, which is best kept trapped in the glass rather than given off and lost to the general

All of these are sensibly shaped wine glasses. The Paris goblet on the left is versatile and inexpensive. The 'tulip' on its right is perhaps a little more elegant and would easily double as a glass for sparkling wine, for which the flûte *is specifically designed. On the right is the traditional sherry copita which would do for any fortified wine, or for brandy.*

atmosphere. To this end, glasses should be filled no more than two-thirds (preferably half) full, and have a bowl shape that narrows towards the rim. That way, the vapour will collect in the space between the wine's surface and the rim of the glass, ready to be enjoyed by the drinker. Examples of sensibly designed glasses are shown here. There is no correlation between sensible design in a wine glass and price. Some of the most expensive, heavily cut crystal glasses boasted by glassware departments of stores are quite useless for savouring wine – and one of the most useful shapes, the Paris goblet, costs relatively little.

Contrary to what glassware manufacturers would have us believe, there is no need to have a wide range of glasses of different shapes and sizes for different wines. The same glass will do perfectly well for most wines, whether they are red or white, sweet or dry, special or everyday. If you are serving two wines of the same colour at the same time, it does help to serve them in slightly different glasses though, for obvious reasons. If you are serving a very alcoholic wine, such as sherry or port, it is wise, but not necessary, to serve them in slightly smaller glasses, such as are also shown here.

There is also a tradition that sparkling wines and champagne be served in tall *flûtes* so that the bubbles do not escape too quickly. However, many of them are designed so that the bouquet of vapour cannot be savoured very easily, and you should be comforted by the fact that even fizz tastes fine in an ordinary wine glass. Only the saucer-shaped *coupes* are a bit awkward, as they encourage the bubbles to make an over-hasty exit and can easily topple over.

Keep all wine glasses very clean. After washing, rinse them thoroughly in hot water so that they will not be tainted by traces of detergent, which can make a fizzy wine look like a still one. Fine glasses should ideally be kept upright to avoid damage to the rim, but if you do store your glasses upside down, make sure that they have at least one hour right side up to dispel any stale air or taste of shelf before pouring wine into them.

QUESTIONS AND ANSWERS

Q. How do you open a bottle of champagne or sparkling wine?

A. Hold the bottle at 45 degrees to maximize the surface area from which the bubbles can escape. Take off the foil and carefully untwist the wire muzzle. Wrap a dry napkin round the bottle neck and gently twist the bottle off the cork (not the other way round, in case the cork breaks). This way, there will be only the gentlest of pops, very little wine lost and no danger to eyes.

Q. What is decanting?

A. Pouring wine from the bottle into another glass container. Traditionally this is something along the lines of the decanters shown here, but a glass jug or ordinary carafe would do.

Q. Should one decant wine?

A. Decanting is necessary only in wines that are sufficiently old and grand to have formed a deposit, yet are not so ancient and fragile (as in wines more than 50 years old) that exposure to air should be kept to an absolute minimum, even at the risk of chewing a mouthful of sediment along with the last glass of wine. For any other sort of wine, it is a matter of personal choice. If you have a particularly beautiful decanter you want to show off, or particularly ordinary wine whose origins you wish to conceal, then decanting may seem a good idea. If the whole business seems just a bit too complicated, then be consoled by the fact that many wine experts are unconvinced about the advantages of decanting. Exposure to air may release a bit more vapour and therefore pleasure, but this can

be done by simply swirling the glasses once the wine has been poured, without risking the dissipation of the precious bouquet too soon. The more body a wine has, the better it can stand up to decanting. Most sweeter sherries and ports can be kept in a decanter for up to a month.

A collection of decanters ancient and modern, though any glass vessel – even a jug – would do.

26

Q. How soon before drinking a wine should you open it?
A. Some people strongly believe in letting open bottles 'breathe' for a couple of hours before serving them. However, it is difficult to see how much effect air can have on the tiny surface area of wine thus allowed in contact with it. Sometimes off-odours can collect as a pocket of stale air between wine and cork known as 'bottle stink', but this is easily dissipated as the wine is poured vigorously into glasses.
Q. How long will wine keep in an opened bottle?
A. It depends on the wine and on how much of it is left. The more full-bodied a wine, the more it can withstand exposure to air and vice versa. It is the mixture of air and wine that is dangerous – because it eventually turns the wine to vinegar – so wine will keep best in a stoppered container that is not much larger than the volume left over. A stock of empty half-bottles, half-litres, screwcap tonic bottles and smaller bottles as served on planes and trains is therefore useful to households too small to consume a whole bottle at a sitting so that leftovers can be poured into whichever is most appropriate. If it is not possible to find a smaller bottle, then the wine will start to taste unpleasantly stale after one to five days depending on how much body it has. Wine boxes are useful because they contain self-deflating bags that let wine out but no air in. Their contents are rarely quite as fresh as those of a bottle, but they start to taste decidedly stale only after several months rather than several days. (See page 37 for more on wine boxes.) It is possible to buy special stoppers for sparkling wines once opened.
Q. What is 'bouquet'?
A. This rather fanciful-sounding word means the intricate smell that develops as a wine matures. It contrasts with the word 'aroma' which is usually used to describe the fresher, simpler smell of a young wine that derives straight from the grapes without the advantage of maturation.

Q. What does 'corked' mean?

A. The term stems from the time when the cork weevil commonly burrowed its way through corks to spoil the wine. Nowadays 'corked' and 'corky' are used fairly interchangeably to describe a wine that is musty and indisputably nasty to smell. The terms have nothing to do with little bits of cork floating in a wine.

Q. What happens when a wine is 'oxidized'?

A. This can happen either in a bottle by accident or by leaving a glass out in the air too long. The air acts on the wine to turn it brown and make it taste stale and flat. 'Maderized', i.e. rather like Madeira, means much the same thing.

In the Restaurant

Q. When the waiter presents a bottle I have ordered, what is the procedure?

A. Look at the label to make sure it is exactly what you ordered, especially the vintage. If you ordered the sort of wine sufficiently grand that the vintage matters, and you have been given a much poorer or younger one, then you are justified in asking for a replacement, or a reduction.

Q. What should happen when a waiter offers a taste of a wine in a restaurant?

A. This outmoded custom stems from a time when wine varied much more from bottle to bottle. It gave the host the chance to check that a wine was in good condition before it was served to his guests. Now it simply allows you to check that the wine has no serious fault (*not* whether you like it or not). It is a bit absurd, since very few waiters give you the chance to taste a second bottle, which has just the same chance of being faulty, i.e. about one per cent.

   If you feel uncomfortable about the tasting ritual, simply

When the waiter shows you the bottle, you can check that the wine (particularly the vintage) is exactly what you ordered.

ask the waiter to pour for everyone. If you have got one of those rare bad bottles, it is not asking too much for him to whisk all the glasses away. Otherwise, glance at the wine to make sure it is not cloudy (see page 15) and then swirl and sniff as outlined on page 13. If after this you feel like drinking the wine then a) it can't be seriously out of condition and b) you can treat yourself to this optional extra as a host's perk if you wish. On drinking the wine, you may feel it is too sweet or dry for your taste, or possibly even too acid or too lightweight or too tannic for you. These judgements are usually too subjective to warrant sending a wine back. Only if a wine is suffering from one of the faults mentioned or is 'corked' or 'oxidized' (above) can both the restaurateur and yourself agree that it is so out of condition it should be sent back (eventually to the supplier, who will refund the restaurateur).

Q. Should the bottle be opened at the table?

A. A good wine waiter will open all bottles, even house wine, in front of his customers to prove to them there has been no substitution. The grander the wine, the greater your right to insist on this point.

Q. How much wine should be ordered for each person?

A. Your calculations will have to take personal habits into account, but half a bottle a head at lunchtime and a whole one in the evening would be generous.

Q. How many glasses to a bottle?

A. Six generous or eight perfectly adequate ones.

Q. If one of the party is eating fish and another meat, what wine should be ordered?

A. Anything you want! Perhaps something from the vast range of fairly full-bodied whites such as those from Burgundy, Rioja, California or Australia or a light, fairly crisp red such as a Beaujolais, *vin de pays* or inexpensive Italian, or any dryish rosé.

SERVING WINE

Q. Is it unhealthy to drink lots of different sorts of wines at one 'sitting'?

A. No. Although mixing grape and grain (e.g. wine or cognac with beer or whisky) is supposed to be particularly taxing to the system, different wines together should not bring a hangover, but rather a greater understanding of the subject. One simple way towards healthy wine drinking is to alternate sips of wine with water.

Q. Do cheap wines cause more of a hangover than expensive ones?

A. This was true a decade ago, but the majority of today's inexpensive wines are made sufficiently well to minimize the after-effects.

Q. How many different wines should be served at a dinner party?

A. One wine will do, especially if no one is really interested in wine except for its alcohol content. On the other hand, if wine is served as an aperitif (for example, champagne or dry white) and digestif (for example, port), as well as especially to complement each course, or even another related wine served concurrently, then as many as seven different wines could be served with one meal. It can be fun to compare two different wines from the same grape or same property. If this seems too fiddly, and uses up too many glasses, consider the fact that a single wine chosen especially for a particular course shows much more consideration on the part of the host.

TEMPERATURE

Q. What is the right temperature for white wines?

A. The warmer a food or drink, the more vapour is released

and the more messages it can send to the brain. The fuller bodied a wine, the more difficult it is to release the vapour. It makes sense therefore not to overchill a good full-bodied white such as a white Burgundy. Very light, aromatic wines such as some Muscats and German Rieslings can take chilling much better. Try to judge the 'body' of a wine before deciding how much to chill it, though bear in mind that overchilling is the ideal solution with a white wine that has a pretty unpleasant smell.

Q. How do you chill wines?

A. An hour or two in the door of the refrigerator is the best way. A speedy alternative is 10–15 minutes in an ice bucket or

The fastest way to chill a bottle is to surround it with icy water.

any receptacle big enough to hold the bottle with a mixture of water and ice (much better than a bucketful of ice cubes alone, which puts only a fraction of the bottle in contact with the cooling agent). A spell in the deep freeze works at about the same speed, although it is important not to leave a bottle in there by mistake, as the wine will freeze and push the cork out or even break the bottle.

Q. What is the right temperature for red wines?

A. The traditional answer is 'room' temperature, but wines served at the same temperature as some centrally heated rooms would rapidly turn to vinegar. At least a wine that is too cool can be rescued by cupping the bowl of the glass in a

Most red wines are best at the temperature of an unheated room.

warm hand, but a wine that becomes too warm can spoil beyond redemption. Red wines are traditionally served warmer than whites partly because they tend to be less naturally aromatic and fuller bodied, and therefore have to be encouraged to give off their vapour, and partly because they are more likely to contain tannin (see page 18). Tannin tastes even more unpleasantly obvious at low temperatures, so a red such as a claret or a Barolo from Italy should be served warmer than a light-bodied, low-tannin wine such as a Beaujolais or Valpolicella. Wines such as these can happily take a bit of chilling, especially in the summer, and are some of the world's most versatile wines as regards the temperature at which they are served and the foods that can be enjoyed with them.

Q. How can red wine be warmed up in a hurry?

A. Probably the most effective way is to pour the wine and warm up each glass by cupping the bowl in the hand. Those who feel wary of asking their guests to 'warm-it-yourself' can put the bottle somewhere warmish but not hot (certainly not on a radiator!). If a wine is robust enough to take decanting, pouring it into a decanter that was previously filled with hot water is another effective method.

Q. What happens to wines that are kept in the refrigerator too long?

A. A complex white that is kept in the refrigerator for more than a week tends to lose its complexity, and this is particularly true of sparkling wines.

KEEPING AND STORING WINE

Q. Does all wine improve with age?

A. Only about 10 per cent of all wine made improves with age, but it is that 10 per cent about which most is written and

spoken. Everyday table wine, *vin de table*, *Tafelwein*, *vino da tavola* and the like gets worse rather than better after a year in bottle and loses the fresh fruity quality that is its greatest asset. However, most claret is built to last for years and sometimes decades, as are many red Burgundies and red Rhône wines and reds from Piedmont such as Barolo. Most reds above the basic level of quality, such as Rioja and Chianti, should become more interesting for the first few years after they were bottled. Fewer white wines than reds are made to develop complexity with age, but the better examples made from Chardonnay and Riesling grapes (such

Bottles to be kept for more than three months should be placed on their sides.

as fine white Burgundy and great German wines) can continue to develop for years without losing their fruitiness. Most sparkling wines are made to be drunk young, though some people like the rather faded, biscuity taste of old champagne. Most fortified wines, other than vintage port and finest Madeira which can last for 50 years, are sold when they are ready to drink.

Q. What happens when a wine ages?

A. No one is quite certain, but what does seem clear is that a concentrated young wine which spends a bit of time in new oak barrels to add new flavours and more tannin is the most likely sort of wine to last. As the wine ages the tannin that was so evident when it was young starts to fade and the complex flavours drawn from the soil via the vine roots start to knit together to produce something much more interesting than the crude young wine.

Q. What is the best way to store wine?

A. If a bottle is to be kept for more than three months it should be kept horizontal so that the wine keeps the cork wet and airtight.

Q. In what conditions should wine be stored?

A. Store wine away from strong light, which tends to oxidize it over long periods (watch out for bottles stored under neon lights in shops for long periods of time) and at a fairly constant temperature. The cooler it is kept, the more slowly it will develop, which is why great cellars are fairly chilly. It is very important not to let the wine get too hot – no more than 20°C (68°F) – or it will start to turn to vinegar. Humidity will not harm the wine, but it may spoil the labels.

Q. Where is the best place to keep wine in a house or flat without a cellar?

A. Unused fireplaces are usually cool, well-insulated and fairly dark. Under the stairs can satisfy most criteria, though bottles with sediment do not take kindly to being jolted by

Anywhere cool and fairly dark will do for your 'cellar'.

constant vibration. A spare bedroom that is kept unheated could be useful, or even a spare chest of drawers in a cool place. Take care to distance your wine from any direct source of heat such as a boiler.

THE PACKAGING

Q. Why is wine put into glass bottles stoppered with corks?
A. Glass imparts no flavour to the wine and the cork, if kept wet, provides an airtight seal that can last for at least 30 years (after which some great châteaux carefully re-cork their wines).
Q. Will wine from a box, can or plastic bottle taste worse than glass-bottled?
A. Provided the wine does not stay in any of these materials for more than a few months there should be no ill effects.

Wine boxes contain self-deflating foil pouches with taps operated by valves that let in no air to spoil the wine. In theory, wine should keep for four months in these boxes. In fact, the technology is still being developed and one or two months seem a safer current maximum.

Q.   What clues are given by the shape of a bottle?

A.   Probably the most common bottle shape is that shown in A, B and C below, for Burgundy, Loire, Rhône, Burgundy-style Rioja and many other wines around the world, especially those based on Chardonnay and Pinot Noir grapes.

Any wine from Bordeaux (D,E), a claret-style Rioja (F), most Italian wines, and many wines based on Cabernet-Sauvignon grapes (G) grown around the world come in bottles with a characteristic shoulder.

The height of the German bottle (J) has been reduced over the years to accommodate space-conscious retailers. Most wines based on Germanic grape varieties, such as English wine (L), are put into this shape. Alsace winemakers use a taller version (K).

Bottles of unusual shape (H, I) are very popular in Italy.

Q. What clues are given by the colour of glass?

A. Very dark glass is in general used for very fine wines designed for a long life, such as vintage port, great claret and great Italian reds. Most bottles come in various shades of green, with fine white Burgundy being most often bottled in a lovely yellow-green colour the French call *feuille morte* or 'dead leaf'. Brown glass is commonly used by the Italians. If a German bottle is green it will usually contain Mosel, and if it is brown it will contain Rhine wine or hock from a region such as the Rheingau, Rheinhessen or Rheinpfalz. If a white Bordeaux is put into green glass it will usually be dry, while the sweet ones such as Sauternes are usually bottled in clear glass.

Q. What size is the average wine bottle?

A. 70cl and 75cl are the most common capacities and these should always be marked on the label. Most American, Australian and South African bottlers use the larger size (more generous by all of seven per cent) and their counterparts elsewhere are being urged to do so.

Q. Are bigger bottles always better value?

A. No. Bottles containing 1.5 litres or the equivalent of two bottles are known as magnums and carry a supplement if they contain fine wine because this is thought to be the optimum size for maturation. Wine matures faster in a smaller container, so half-bottles should be drunk before bottles. They are not cheap though because of the extra labour and material costs involved. However, good retailers will normally offer their customers some financial incentive to buy larger bottles of most basic wines.

WINE, ALCOHOL AND HEALTH

Q. How can one tell from the label how strong a wine is?

A. Unlike average capacity and provenance, alcohol content

is not yet required information on wine labels. As well as the Californians and Australians, the Italians are usually good at giving this particular vital statistic, sometimes called Gradi, or even 'G', meaning percentage of alcohol by volume. Alcoholic strength for wine will always be measured this way, although sometimes a label may state, say, 12° or 12 GL (Gay-Lussac) instead of 12%. Most supermarkets do declare the alcohol by volume on their own wine labels.

Q. How much alcohol does wine contain?

A. A wine can contain anything from 6–16% perfectly naturally, by the action of yeast on the sugar in the grapes, though fortified wines can be even stronger (see below). Among the least alcoholic wines are many German wines, especially sweeter, late picked specimens from the Mosel, and Asti Spumante which are only about 7% alcohol. Vinho Verde and New Zealand wines are often about 9 or 10%; basic French table wine is 10 or 11%; claret is 11–12%; Burgundy, Spanish and Australian wine can be as strong as 13%; some Rhône wines exceed this, as do many from California. Some of the naturally strongest wines come from Italy. Barolo must be at least 13% alcohol, while Amarone della Valpolicella, made from dried Valpolicella grapes, can sometimes be as strong as 16%.

Q. How strong are fortified wines?

A. Light dry sherries sold in Spain may be only 15%, as are most Montillas and sherry-style wines from Cyprus. Most sherry is exported at just under 18%, however, as are the cheaper qualities of port. Old tawny and, especially, vintage port may be as strong as 20%, as are superior Madeiras. Most vermouths are just under 18%.

Q. What is the alcohol content of wines relative to beer and spirits?

A. Beer varies in strength between 4 and 6% while most spirits are 40% (the equivalent of 70° on the old proof scale).

The medical shorthand for guidance on safe alcohol consumption is that 'a glass of wine' is equivalent to half-a-pint of beer or a measure of spirits but, as we have seen, this measure is not exactly rigorous. The safest way to moderate consumption is to be wary of very alcoholic wines and to alternate more than two or three glasses of wine with water or soft drinks.

Q. Is wine healthier than other alcoholic drinks?

A. Wine is less potent than spirits and less fattening than beer. Dry wines low in alcohol are the wines most suitable for slimmers, who should avoid both the strong and the sweet. Wine also contains small amounts of vitamins and minerals which were thought by one French doctor to be sufficiently significant to warrant a book prescribing a wine for every ailment. It should be remembered however that wine should be treated with the caution appropriate to all drinks containing alcohol.

How to Read a Label

The most important thing to identify on a wine label is the wine's ranking on the ladder of quality. Wines from outside the EEC have a less carefully defined system but the most basic level in a wine produced in the EEC is table wine, *vin de table* (French), *Tafelwein* (German) or *vino da tavola* (Italian). Just at the top of this category, into which most of the world's basic wines and a few very exciting ones (notably in Italy) fall, are *vin de pays* (French) and *Landwein* (German) which are allowed to add some sort of geographical qualification on to their quality ranking.

Above this level wines become known as 'quality wines'. The two-tier French system is based on *Appellation Contrôlée* (AC), which has become a model for quality designation

systems almost everywhere else other than Germany, which has its own intricate system. The system lays down conditions governing the production of wine in a certain area, and is concerned with aspects such as the exact limits of that area, the grape varieties allowed, the maximum yield allowed per acre and the alcoholic strength of the eventual wine. The authorities allow documentation for an *Appellation Contrôlée* wine only if these conditions have been met. The more specific the area to which the Appellation refers, the better the wine. A wine labelled *Appellation Bordeaux Contrôlée* for instance can come from anywhere in the vast Bordeaux region, whereas an *Appellation Médoc Contrôlée* must come from the Médoc area within it, and one labelled *Appellation*

Type of wine. Blanc de blancs *means "white of whites", which must by law be a white wine made from white grapes*

"French table wine" This basic designation of quality simply means that the wine is from France, not from a particular region and not subject to the strict rules of Appellation Controlée *or* V.D.Q.S.

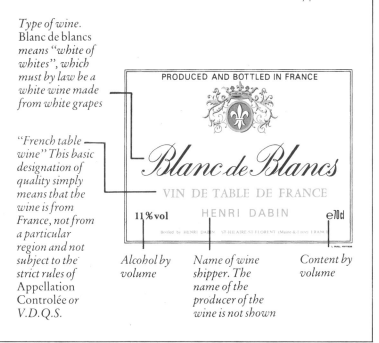

PRODUCED AND BOTTLED IN FRANCE

Blanc de Blancs

VIN DE TABLE DE FRANCE

11 % vol   HENRI DABIN   e 70 cl

Bottled by HENRI DABIN ST HILAIRE ST FLORENT (Maine & Loire) FRANCE

Alcohol by volume

Name of wine shipper. The name of the producer of the wine is not shown

Content by volume

Pauillac Contrôlée must come from the parish of Pauillac in the Médoc. If the label of a wine says VDQS, meaning *Vin Délimité de Qualité Supérieure*, it will belong to the small category just between *vin de pays* and *Appellation Contrôlée*. Once you have worked out that a wine is AC or VDQS, you can tell its geographical origin which also must always be stated on the label.

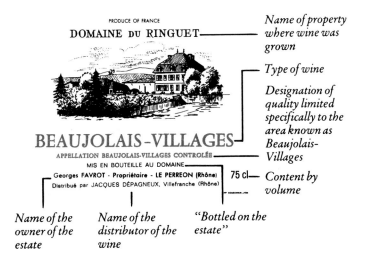

PRODUCE OF FRANCE

DOMAINE DU RINGUET —————— *Name of property where wine was grown*

Type of wine

Designation of quality limited specifically to the area known as Beaujolais-Villages

BEAUJOLAIS-VILLAGES

APPELLATION BEAUJOLAIS-VILLAGES CONTROLÉE —————

MIS EN BOUTEILLE AU DOMAINE

Georges FAVROT · Propriétaire · LE PERREON (Rhône) | 75 cl — *Content by volume*

Distribué par JACQUES DÉPAGNEUX, Villefranche (Rhône)

Name of the owner of the estate · *Name of the distributor of the wine* · *"Bottled on the estate"*

Italy's equivalent of AC is DOC or *Denominazione di Origine Controllata* and works in much the same way – if slightly less effectively. There are disappointing wines that have been awarded the DOC for reasons of local politics, just as some excellent Italian wines have to be labelled simply as *vino da tavola* because they don't conform to the traditions enshrined in the DOC regulations. A very special top category, DOCG, has been introduced for a handful of wines whose 'denomination' is not only checked (*Controllata*) but

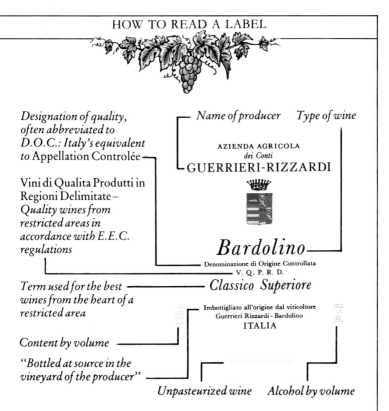

Designation of quality, often abbreviated to D.O.C.: Italy's equivalent to Appellation Controlée

Vini di Qualita Produtti in Regioni Delimitate – Quality wines from restricted areas in accordance with E.E.C. regulations

Term used for the best wines from the heart of a restricted area

Content by volume

"Bottled at source in the vineyard of the producer"

Name of producer   Type of wine

AZIENDA AGRICOLA
dei Conti
GUERRIERI-RIZZARDI

Bardolino
Denominazione di Origine Controllata
V. Q. P. R. D.

Classico Superiore

Imbottigliato all'origine dal viticoltore
Guerrieri Rizzardi - Bardolino
ITALIA

Unpasteurized wine   Alcohol by volume

also guaranteed (*Garantita*)! Other wine regions of the world are stumbling towards similar wine quality designation systems. The South Africans already have their Wines of Origin, the Spaniards their *Denominación de Origen*.

As described on page 92, the Germans superimpose on their geographically inspired labelling another aspect very dear to them – ripeness. The great majority of German wine falls into a category called QbA or *Qualitätswein* just above *Landwein* but below their top wines, called QmP or *Qualitätswein mit Prädikat*. German wines earn a 'predicate', a descriptive term appearing on the label, by having a high level of natural sugar when picked. Kabinett, Spätlese, Auslese, Beerenauslese and Trockenbeerenauslese are 'predicates', listed here in ascending order of sweetness, and will always appear on the label of a QmP wine. If a wine is made from frozen grapes, the word Eiswein may be added to one of these predicates. Austria has a very similar system because the wine industry there is based on Germanic grapes.

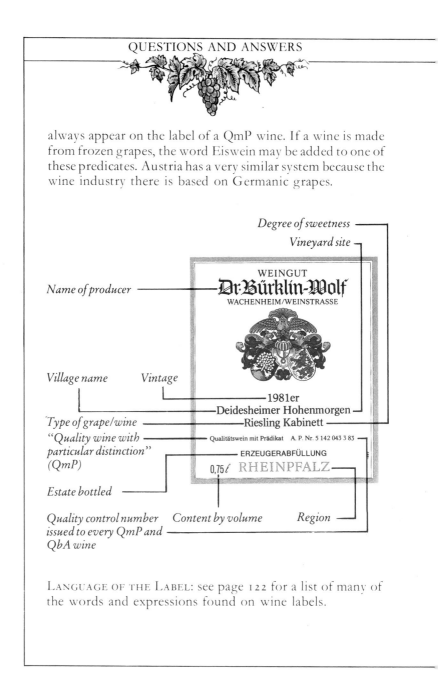

Degree of sweetness

Vineyard site

Name of producer

Village name   Vintage

Type of grape/wine

"Quality wine with particular distinction" (QmP)

Estate bottled

Quality control number issued to every QmP and QbA wine

Content by volume

Region

WEINGUT
Dr. Bürklin-Wolf
WACHENHEIM/WEINSTRASSE

1981er
Deidesheimer Hohenmorgen
Riesling Kabinett
Qualitätswein mit Prädikat   A. P. Nr. 5 142 043 3 83
ERZEUGERABFÜLLUNG
0,75 ℓ   RHEINPFALZ

LANGUAGE OF THE LABEL: see page 122 for a list of many of the words and expressions found on wine labels.

HOW WINE IS MADE

A Year in the Vineyard

The fascinating variety of wine made from grapes (compared to wine made from other fruits) is due to the extraordinary nature of the vine.

In terms of a wine's alcohol level, perhaps the most important thing that happens in the vineyard year is that the sun ripens the grapes sufficiently to produce enough sugar to ferment into alcohol. However, to be transformed into something with the balance and complexity of wine, the grapes must first contain sufficient acids to give zip to the liquid, and they should have a wide variety of trace elements, picked up from the soil via the vine roots, to make up the nuances of flavour. In an established well-drained vineyard, the vine, in its search for moisture, may put down roots as much as 30 feet into the earth, picking up an enormous range of trace elements en route. Another source of flavour, and therefore pleasure, may well be the elements above the ground. Cabernets from certain Californian vineyards taste of the eucalyptus trees around them.

The characteristics of the grape are determined by the vine, the principal varieties of which are outlined on pages 62 to 64. All of these are members of the European family of vines – the mainstays of European wine production. In the late nineteenth century the roots of European vines were attacked, with devastating effect, by the vine pest – phylloxera – accidentally introduced from America. The whole wine business seemed doomed, until it was realized that native American vines would have developed a resistance to

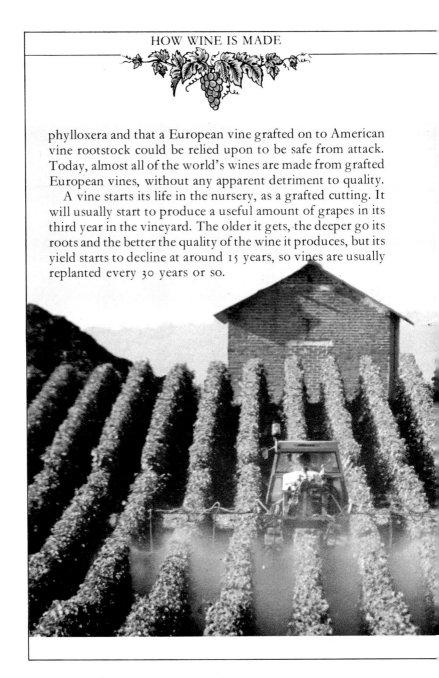

phylloxera and that a European vine grafted on to American vine rootstock could be relied upon to be safe from attack. Today, almost all of the world's wines are made from grafted European vines, without any apparent detriment to quality.

A vine starts its life in the nursery, as a grafted cutting. It will usually start to produce a useful amount of grapes in its third year in the vineyard. The older it gets, the deeper go its roots and the better the quality of the wine it produces, but its yield starts to decline at around 15 years, so vines are usually replanted every 30 years or so.

After every harvest the vineyard is tidied up and allowed a winter dormancy. And it is during this time that the all-important pruning takes place, when the shape and productivity of the vine the following summer is determined by a few careful snips. Late spring sees the first vine shoots, which have to be protected from late frosts. The crucial flowering of the vine takes place in June in the northern hemisphere, and a period of warm settled weather then will mean that the potential quantity is maximized and all the grapes in a given

Spraying against rot and vine disease is a vital part of the lead-up to the vintage. Inset *Minervois, south of France.*

patch will, conveniently, ripen at the same time.

During the summer, both sunshine and moisture are needed. Rain is the traditional source of the latter, but some newer wine regions are simulating rain with, for example, overhead sprays or drips from tubing strung along the wires on which most vines nowadays are trained. This training ensures that the optimum amount of leaf is exposed to the sun's rays so that photosynthesis will take place and result in ripe grapes.

During this ripening period the vine is susceptible to rot and all sorts of diseases – a fact that has brought prosperity to merchants of agricultural chemicals. Some vineyards may be sprayed as often as 20 times in very humid years to keep the grapes healthy.

Some time in the late summer or autumn – between mid-August and late November in the northern hemisphere and February-March in the southern hemisphere – the vine grower has to decide when to pick. As the sugar level increases so does the potential alcohol, though the acid level

Stainless steel now plays a major part in white wine vinification.

declines and rain, rot, hail, frost and other disasters loom. This is the most difficult decision of the vineyard year, with more than an element of risk about it.

Most grapes are still picked by hand rather than mechanical harvesters, but they are gaining ground rapidly, and not just in the new wine regions. There are now three times as many machines in Bordeaux as in California, for instance. Controversy rages as to whether they damage the grapes, or bring advantages because they are quicker and, in hotter regions, can pick at night. It is just possible that the grapes at Château Lafite-Rothschild will one day be picked by machine.

How White Wine is Made

It is not difficult to turn grapes into wine. The winemaker's job is to transform the year's freshly picked grapes into the most appetizing wine possible.

Yeast harbours enzymes. When those enzymes are introduced to sugar they turn it into alcohol – a process called fermentation. In any established vineyard there are thousands of yeasts floating about in the atmosphere, some of which are naturally to be found on the grapeskins. Inside each grape is a high proportion of water, sugar in quantities determined by its ripeness, acids, a wide range of trace elements and the pips. As soon as a grapeskin is broken, the yeast comes into contact with the sugar inside the pulp and fermentation begins. The yeast continues to convert the sugar into alcohol until either it runs out of sugar so that the resulting wine is dry, or it reaches its maximum alcohol production and can do no more, leaving some residual sugar in the wine. Very few yeasts can function in a liquid stronger than 16% alcohol, for example.

Man must have discovered wine simply by leaving freshly

picked grapes in a container – an amphora perhaps? The weight of the grapes on top would have crushed the grapes at the bottom, the juice of which would rapidly have been converted into wine. However, this happy natural process is just a little too haphazard for today's professionals. Wine and air is a potentially dangerous combination, for instance, as anyone who has left a bit of wine in a glass overnight will have noticed. The oxygen in the air acts on the wine, making it taste stale and 'oxidizing' it.

The modern winemaker has sufficient knowledge and equipment to leave as little as possible to chance. Nowadays he will often kill off all the yeasts occurring naturally, by judicious use of the winemaker's antiseptic, sulphur dioxide, and introduce yeasts that have been specially cultivated to work as effectively as possible for the sort of wine required. There are also many ways of keeping the wine's contact with air to a minimum. The whole process of crushing and fermentation can be swathed in a 'blanket' of inert gas, such as nitrogen, which will protect it from harmful oxygen.

When making white wine, he can choose from a range of sophisticated methods for eliminating the harsher, solid parts of the grape. Using one of the many types of press now available, the juice is pressed out of the grape pulp with a degree of delicacy determined by the importance of avoiding any possible taint of astringency from the skins and pips. The harder the grapes are pressed, the more juice, and therefore wine, will be made, but the lower its likely quality. All the little solids that still remain in the juice are usually removed before the fermentation gets going, either by centrifuge or by allowing them to settle out overnight.

In the modern winery, white wines are usually fermented in closed vats made of an inert substance such as stainless steel. Though unromantic, it is hygienic and preserves the fresh fruit flavour so important in most white wines.

The fermentation process is very sensitive to temperature. Yeasts will not function if it is too cold, and they are not effective in extreme heat. This means that in cooler climates winemakers may have to heat the must, the fermenting grape juice, to get at least the first vatful started. Fermentation generates heat, however, so it is sometimes necessary to cool the must as it is fermenting. This is particularly important in the production of white wines whose youthful grape aromas are their most prized quality. The world's winemakers still vary considerably in the temperature they think ideal for fermenting different grapes and will doubtless continue to do so. What is exciting for today's wine drinker, however, is that, with the help of refrigeration coils and tanks which can automatically be sprayed with cooling waters, winemakers are able to control the length and intensity of fermentation by adjusting temperature.

Fermentation can be allowed to stop naturally, leaving residual sugar only if the grapes are very ripe. A more usual technique of making wine sweet, very popular in Germany, is to add sterilized unfermented grape juice to the finished dry wine. Fermentation can also be stopped by the winemaker, either by adding lots more sulphur dioxide or, a more sophisticated method, by suddenly chilling the must and then filtering out any organisms that could threaten to restart fermentation.

MAKING RED AND ROSÉ WINES

In contrast to white, red wine needs one important ingredient – colouring matter. As anyone who has peeled a black grape knows, grape pulp is the same grey-green colour whatever the colour of a grape's skin. The pigments available to turn a wine red are all concentrated in the skin, so it is vital that red wines are fermented in contact with the skins.

The winemaker's first job with red grapes is to separate them from the stalks which make the wine harsh if left in the fermentation vat. Some more traditional winemakers, and those copying them in newer wine regions, may leave a small proportion of the stalks in to add staying power if they feel it is needed, but the crusher-destemmer is usually the first piece of cellar gadgetry to which red grapes are introduced.

Inside the fermentation vat, the skins naturally float to the top of the pulpy mixture fed out of the crusher-destemmer and form a 'cap' that prevents oxygen spoiling the must beneath. If the winemaker wants to extract lots of colouring matter from the skins, he will make sure that the wine is often pumped over this cap, or that it is broken up by hand, or kept submerged by mechanical means.

Grapeskins are a principal source of another important element in red wine – tannin. This is the stewed-tea-like substance that acts as a preservative while long-lasting red wine ages. If a winemaker is working with grapes of a really high quality, he will make sure that sufficient tannin is extracted from the skins during fermentation to keep the wine going strong, to allow time for its more complex fruit-based flavours to emerge in the years to come.

The heat generated by the process of fermentation helps to leech the pigments and tannins out of the skins. Red wines are allowed to ferment at higher temperatures than whites to encourage this, and some winemakers even heat the must.

Red wines are almost always fermented out to make a dry wine, using up all the available sugar, though very alcoholic wines can taste 'sweet'. The must/wine is left in contact with the skins for anything up to three weeks, depending on how dark and tannic the winemaker wants to make the wine. Rosés are traditionally made by leaving the skins in contact with the juice for only a few hours. Winemakers who want to produce a red wine with lots of colour but very little tannin

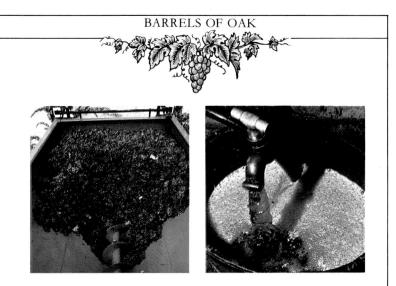

The magic of fermentation transforms blue grapes into foaming crimson wine, the colour coming exclusively from the grapeskins.

use some variant of the technique called *macération carbonique* which involves fermenting red grapes very briefly in a vatful of carbon dioxide, crushing as few grapes as possible. This is very popular in Beaujolais and many areas of southern France.

With the more traditional method, the assorted solids left in the fermentation vat after the wine has been run off are pressed firmly and the resulting liquid fermented to produce ultra-harsh 'press wine', the opposite of the soft, fruity liquid produced by *macération carbonique*. This may be added to give additional body to the wine produced by the initial fermentation, or it may be served up with staff meals to give additional body to the workers.

BARRELS OF OAK

Everyday reds will probably be bottled, like most whites, just a few months after the vintage to preserve their fresh fruity

flavour, but more intense reds are left to pick up extra elements of flavour and tannins from wood. Great red wines and those designed for long ageing may be left for months, sometimes years, to mature in oak – either small barrels or large vats. Different oaks impart different flavours, with American oak giving a sweet suggestion of vanilla and some of the French oaks being rather more subtle.

While the wine is kept in barrel, it is important to keep it moving fairly frequently from one barrel to another so that it does not pick up any harmful bacteria or flavours from the lees in the bottom of the barrel. This process is called 'racking', and may be preceded by 'fining', that is precipitating the tiniest solids by adding a substance that attracts them, such as white of egg. The top châteaux of Bordeaux boast of the number of egg yolks thrown out each year.

In the production of any wine, the blending of different vats, or different barrels, or different grape varieties or even completely different wines is a highly skilled operation and can play a crucial role in determining flavour. It is important to stress that blending can be a noble art and not necessarily a sign of skulduggery.

Sparkling Wines

Not all that sparkles is necessarily great wine, but great sparkling wine offers a uniquely exciting experience.

There are four main methods of putting a sparkle (always carbon dioxide gas) into wine:

Carbonation This, the so-called 'bicycle pump method', is no more sophisticated than simply pumping carbon dioxide into a tankful of wine. It is also used for fizzy soft drinks and achieves a bubble just as crude and short-lived in wine. If a bottle opens with a tremendous gush and then subsides

rapidly into a wine that is almost flat, then the carbonation method was probably used.

CUVE CLOSE Most wines should be good enough to warrant this particular sparkling treatment at the very least. A vat or *cuve* of wine has a mixture of sugar and yeast added to it. The yeast provokes a second fermentation which produces alcohol but which, as in all fermentations, gives off carbon dioxide as a side-effect. (Cellar workers are warned to beware putting their head inside a vat of fermenting must of any sort. So much carbon dioxide is given off it could make them faint.) The vats used for making *cuve close* wines are sealed and the gas therefore forced to dissolve in the wine. Provided the wine is bottled under pressure, the bubbles will stay in the bottle until it is opened. This is the most common way of making wine fizzy and is used for most French sparklers labelled *vin mousseux*. This is also known as the tank or Charmat method.

TRANSFER The more contact there is between the lees of the second fermentation and the wine, the more character the sparkling wine will have. The transfer method uses this by bottling the mixture of wine, yeast and sugar, and allowing the second fermentation to take place in bottle. The wine is rested for a time afterwards before the sediment is filtered out under pressure and the wine put into another bottle. This technique is popular in Germany, where *Sekt* is made.

MÉTHODE CHAMPENOISE The 'champagne method' is the most involved of all, but should result in the finest, longest-lasting fizz. The mixture of wine, yeast and sugar is put into the bottle in which it is eventually sold which is stored horizontally. The second fermentation takes place, leaving the sediment on the underside where it can stay for years, adding richness and complexity to the wine. The bottle is gradually shaken and moved so that it is vertical and upside down, with the sediment resting in the neck. When the neck

The process of taking out the cork to allow the sediment to spring out in a frozen plug is called dégorgement.

is frozen and the bottle opened, the sediment pops out in a neat plug. Once the bottle has been topped up with a mixture of wine and sugar, a new cork is inserted. A wine labelled Brut has very little sugar added, while one labelled Sec or Dry has a bit more and a Rich is positively sweet.

These methods rely heavily on the quality of the still wine used as a base. It is generally accepted that the finest base wines come from the Chardonnay and Pinot vines of the Champagne region in north-east France, and it is only these wines, made bubbly by the *méthode champenoise*, that may be called champagne. Everything else has to be called, rather primly, 'sparkling wine'. Most champagne is very dry and labelled simply with the name of the 'house' that made it. About one bottle in five is wine from a single year, but blending is the key to champagne-making and the great majority of the wine is NV, meaning non-vintage: a blend of wines from different years.

Any French sparkling wine that is allowed to put Appellation Contrôlée on the label will have been made by

the *méthode champenoise*. Some of the finest and lightest come from Chenin Blanc grapes grown in Saumur and Vouvray, both in the Loire, though there are some good Crémants (which has come to be synonymous with sparkling wine but should be slightly less fizzy) from Alsace and Bourgogne in Burgundy. Blanquette de Limoux, Clairette de Die and Saint Péray are all very creditable AC sparklers from southern France, though the biggest sellers tend to be non-AC branded wines – usually made by the *cuve close* method.

Spain produces enormous quantities of *méthode champenoise* wine in Catalonia. It has a fuller flavour than champagne but can be very well-made and good value. Enormous progress has also been made in northern Italy, now making some very fine *méthode champenoise* dry white wine. Almost all wine regions turn out some sparkling wine, of varying quality. The Russians drink huge quantities of it, and California has seen enormous investment over the last few years – most of it from Europe, and much of it from Champagne!

FORTIFIED WINES

There is an enormous range of drinks that are made by 'fortifying' wine with alcohol, added either after fermentation to the dry wine or during fermentation to the must while it is still sweet. Some of these are so strongly flavoured and artfully concocted that they are only very distant relations of wine. These are the principal fortified wines (about 18% alcohol by volume):

SHERRY Spain's most famous wine comes from white Palomino grapes grown at the southernmost tip of the country, around Jerez. Grape spirit is added to the wine only after fermentation is complete and the strong, dry liquid is left to mature in traditional wooden casks in the *bodegas* of the

sherry towns. The lighter, more delicate wines are encouraged to form *flor*, a protective growth that covers the
wine's surface like a thin layer of soggy bread, while the
richer wines are allowed to oxidize, gaining colour and the
characteristic 'flat' taste of sherry. Most commercial sherries
are carefully blended and then sweetened, by adding a very
strong, sweet, raisiny wine, before bottling. Fino and
Manzanilla are the palest, lightest and driest, of which
Manzanilla is supposed to have an ultra-appetizing suggestion of brine. Amontillado is medium in body, medium dark
and medium dry (though it is possible to find dry Amontil-
lados to which no sweetening wine has been added, and they
are tinglingly delicious). Oloroso is darker and richer still,
while Cream sherries are the sweetest of all. Pale Creams have
the sweetness of a dark Cream and the colour of a Fino.
Montilla near Jerez produces wines that are very similar to
sherry, without quite the weight. Sherry-style wines are made
all over the world, with notable success in Cyprus and South
Africa and great ingenuity in Australia and California.

PORT, epitomizing the other major style of fortified wine, is
always strong and relatively sweet because the alcohol is
added during fermentation. Port is made from red and white
grapes grown high up in the valley of the river Douro in
Portugal and usually matured in port 'lodges', low ware-
houses near the mouth of the river at Oporto. Ruby port is
young fiery crimson wine that has spent up to five years in
cask. As it ages, it becomes browner and paler in colour and
softer in flavour. An Old Tawny, the port most commonly
drunk by the port wine trade, may be anything from eight to
40 years old, with the optimum for flavour being between 15
and 20 years. Most cheaper ports labelled Tawny are given a
tawny hue simply by adding some White port to young
Ruby. White port varies in sweetness from off-dry to very
sweet, but is difficult to find outside Portugal. Much of the

The sherry vineyards around Jerez in southern Spain were probably the last to become mechanized.

port that is exported today is about five to eight years old, styled as either a superior Ruby or a moderately old Tawny. Most venerated of all, however, is Vintage port, a wine made from the best wines of a single exceptionally good year bottled early and left for decades to develop to concentrated magnificence. Such bottles are usually very simply labelled and have been matured so long that they call for a decanter to separate the wine from the sediment. However, more than 95 per cent of all port sold today has no sediment and can be poured straight from the bottle. Some port shippers bottle wines from less good vintages a little later in their development so that they can be drunk just five years or so after the vintage. These wines, usually labelled much more flashily than Vintage port, often giving great prominence to the year, are called Late Bottled Vintage or Vintage Character port.

MADEIRA is a rich wine made on the Portuguese island of the same name. It is traditionally heated up to more than $37°C$ ($100°F$) during the production process. This gives it a 'burnt' flavour, and an exceptionally long life. Sercial and Verdelho are the driest, Bual is very plummy and Malmsey is the sweetest and darkest.

VERMOUTH is the generic term for all those fortified wines, dry and white or sweet and red, that sell in such huge quantities under a brand name such as Martini, Cinzano and Riccadonna. The basic principle of production is to strip base wines of flavour and colour, add alcohol and flavourings, often herb-based, and possibly sweetening wines.

PRINCIPAL GRAPE VARIETIES

WHITE

Chardonnay Smoky dry, fairly full-bodied wines that last and mature well. Classic for white Burgundy such as Chablis, Montrachet and Mâcon but also grown extensively in California and increasingly in all fine wine regions.

Riesling The other great white that can develop wonderful complexity with age. Flowery fragrant when young, sharper overtones when older. The grape of all great German wines and known elsewhere as Rhine Riesling and Johannisberg or White Riesling. Italian, Laski and Olasz types not related.

Sauvignon Blanc Very popular as a crisp dry white for early consumption. Smells of under-ripe fruit. Known as Fumé Blanc in California. At its most typical in Sancerre and Pouilly-Fumé.

Chenin Blanc Most wines are medium dry and slightly honeyed. Best established on the Loire at Vouvray and Anjou but commonly sold in the newer wine regions, especially South Africa where it is also known as Steen.

Burgundy grapes – Chardonnay (left) and Pinot Noir (right).

Muscadet The grape of the very dry and tart wine.
Muscat A grape producing all degrees of sweetness and strength, and many local variants such as Moscato, Moscatel, Muscadelle.
Müller-Thurgau Germany's most widely planted grape, turning out Riesling-inspired wines that are noticeably lower in acidity and character and must be drunk young.
Gewürztraminer Exotically perfumed grape producing relatively high-alcohol wines. Known best in Alsace but planted in many wine regions outside France.
Pinot Blanc Everyday slightly Chardonnay-like dry whites. Grown notably in Alsace, and northern Italy as Pinot Bianco.
Sylvaner High in acidity and often fairly low in fruit. Basic Alsace and known as Silvaner in Germany.

RED
Cabernet Sauvignon The classic claret grape is dry, tannic when young and long-lived, with an aroma of blackcurrants and/or cedarwood. This grape has travelled furthest and most successfully from its homeland, Bordeaux, especially

Médoc and Graves. Now the most respected red grape in places as diverse as California, Australia, Greece and France's southerly wine regions.

Pinot Noir Providing a nice contrast with Cabernet Sauvignon, the classic red grape of Burgundy responds badly to being transplanted. At its finest it produces wines that are rich and heavily perfumed, with the scent of raspberries when young and truffles or violets when more mature. Examples include Chambertin, Beaune, Nuits-St-Georges.

Syrah This grape makes dense, concentrated, very dry wines in the northern Rhône including Hermitage and some Côtes-du-Rhône, and much softer, sweeter, looser styles in Australia where it is known as Shiraz.

Merlot Across the river from Médoc and Graves, the 'right bank' Bordeaux areas of St Emilion and Pomerol rely heavily on the plummy, spicy Merlot. Also grown on the West Coast of the USA and in northern Italy.

Cabernet Franc A lighter cousin of Cabernet Sauvignon grown extensively in the Loire, Bordeaux and northern Italy. Found in Chinon and many Italian Cabernets.

Gamay The light-bodied, crisp, very fruity grape of Beaujolais, designed to be drunk young.

Nebbiolo Deep-coloured, tannic, pruney grape grown in Piedmont in northern Italy for wines like Barolo and Barbaresco.

Sangiovese The chief red grape of Chianti with an attractively open fruity flavour.

Grenache Sweet, light-coloured red, relatively high in alcohol. Found in Châteauneuf, Côtes-du-Rhône and Rioja.

THE RANGE AVAILABLE

INTRODUCTION

Vines grow all over the place, even in British gardens. Anyone whose house is festooned with Virginia creeper can see that the vine family is a large and varied one. Wild vines flourish worldwide but are grown specifically to produce wine only in the temperate regions shown overleaf.

If a vine is planted too close to the equator it will, as in some South American vineyards, produce two crops of mediocre quality a year rather than one good one. However, some spots cool enough to allow the vine a restorative winter dormancy will be so inhospitable that there is too little sunshine to ripen the grapes. This is evident in parts of the UK as some British vine-growers know to their cost.

The vine is most at home, therefore, in a climate that has cool winters and relatively warm summers with some rain to swell the grapes. During the winter the only disaster that weather can bring is an exceptional frost so severe that it affects the next year's growth below the ground. A much gentler frost in spring can freeze off the year's potential fruit if the vine has already flowered. A really dull summer and autumn may leave the grapes unripe, while hail on ripe grapes can shatter them, and too much rain in the weeks before the harvest can, literally, dilute the quality of the crop.

More than 50 countries produce wine in some quantity. Some of them, such as Belgium and India, are at the climatological limits of cultivation and produce a small amount that is exported only by mistake. The most important

wine-producing countries in terms of quantity produced are Italy, France, the USSR, Spain and Argentina. Of these, France produces by far the widest range.

Within France alone there is enormous variation in climate. The wines of the north, such as Muscadet and Vouvray made along the Loire, show that when the vine is raised relatively far from the equator the resultant wines are light in body and high in acidity. In the south, however, around Avignon in Côtes-du-Rhône and Châteauneuf-du-

WINE-GROWING AREAS OF THE WORLD

Most of the world's wine is produced in countries that lie in the two temperate zones shown here. They include:

France	Morocco
Italy	Algeria
Germany	Tunisia
Spain	Cyprus
Portugal	Greece
Austria	Turkey
Hungary	Lebanon
Yugoslavia	USA
Bulgaria	Mexico
Romania	Argentina
USSR	Chile
British Isles	Australia
Luxembourg	New Zealand
Switzerland	South Africa

Pape country, the wines show how much more body and less acidity a little more sunshine brings. The amount of acidity and body in a wine should be enough to give strong clues as to the sort of climate from which it came.

Although each wine region has its own sort of climate, each vineyard has its own special weather conditions, shaped by factors such as altitude, elevation, proximity to woods and exposure to winds. This is known as its 'microclimate', an impressive name to drop in wine circles.

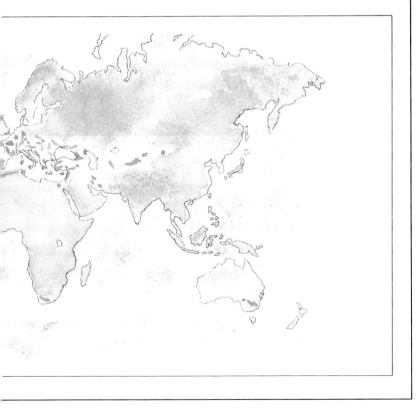

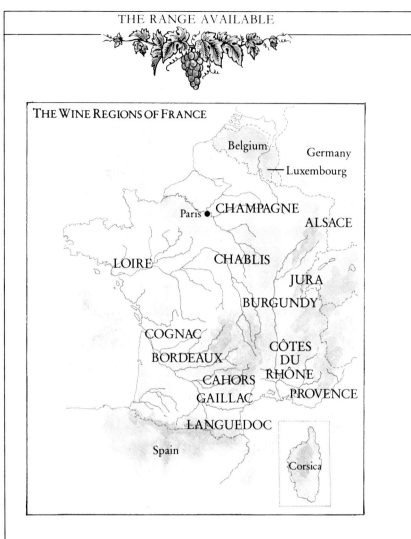

THE WINE REGIONS OF FRANCE

Belgium

Germany

Luxembourg

Paris ● CHAMPAGNE

ALSACE

LOIRE

CHABLIS

JURA

BURGUNDY

COGNAC

BORDEAUX

CÔTES
DU
RHÔNE

CAHORS

GAILLAC

PROVENCE

LANGUEDOC

Spain

Corsica

BORDEAUX

Bordeaux is the most revered wine region in the world. This is partly because it produces more good-quality wine than any other, partly because its wines live considerably longer

than most (though a decreasing proportion of them are now allowed to). It is also because its principal grape varieties are planted all over the world, especially in the newer wine regions. Bordeaux wines are therefore seen as the all-important models by most winemakers and wine consumers.

This large region's most important wine is red Bordeaux, which has been called claret in Britain ever since the light wines of western France were first imported centuries ago (then called *clairet*, meaning 'pale wine'). More connoisseurs enthuse about claret than any other wine. It is dry and not too alcoholic (about 11%) which makes it very digestible and easy to drink with food. It is also quite tart and relatively high in tannin, which makes it essential to drink it with food. Most claret would make about as good an aperitif as a glass of lemon juice mixed with stewed tea.

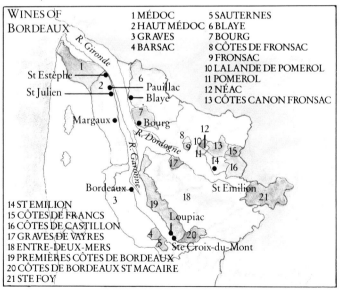

WINES OF BORDEAUX

1 MÉDOC
2 HAUT MÉDOC
3 GRAVES
4 BARSAC
5 SAUTERNES
6 BLAYE
7 BOURG
8 CÔTES DE FRONSAC
9 FRONSAC
10 LALANDE DE POMEROL
11 POMEROL
12 NÉAC
13 CÔTES CANON FRONSAC
14 ST EMILION
15 CÔTES DE FRANCS
16 CÔTES DE CASTILLON
17 GRAVES DE VAYRES
18 ENTRE-DEUX-MERS
19 PREMIÈRES CÔTES DE BORDEAUX
20 CÔTES DE BORDEAUX ST MACAIRE
21 STE FOY

R. Gironde
St Estèphe
St Julien
Margaux
Pauillac
Blaye
Bourg
R. Dordogne
R. Garonne
Bordeaux
St Emilion
Loupiac
Ste Croix-du-Mont

The most famous clarets come from the two best-known red wine areas on the left bank of the Gironde, the Médoc and Graves. Most of the wine produced here comes from a

Microclimate, the climate of a tiny patch of land, is vital. The vineyards of Château Lafite-Rothschild in the background are perfect for fine claret, but the midground would be far too wet. Inset Vintage at Château Latour, just down the road.

specific 'château', which is the name of the property and the name of the administrative building around which the vines are planted (even if it is only a farm shack) and the name of the wine it produces from these, and only these, vines.

The system is very neat, in contrast to the perplexing disorder of Burgundy, and was made even easier to understand in 1855 when an official classification of the 60-odd most reputable Châteaux was drawn up. This ranking is

The vineyards of St Emilion are much smaller, gentler and prettier than those of the Médoc on the opposite side of the river.

rather like the football league tables but has remained much more constant and is in use today. The 'first growths' or *premiers crus* are Châteaux Lafite, Latour, Margaux, Mouton-Rothschild and Haut-Brion, the only Graves property grafted on to all the Médocs in 1855, presumably because it had already established a fine reputation. (There is mention of it as early as Pepys's diaries.)

The *premiers crus* are the star wines and such is their international fame that they cost about twice as much as even a second growth, such as Châteaux Ducru-Beaucaillou or Léoville Lascases, even though these particular wines may well be almost as good. A label of a Médoc wine that says simply Grand Cru Classé may be a third, fourth or fifth growth. The other top properties of the Graves region now have their own classification, and there is a useful group of

Châteaux just 'below' fifth growths called bourgeois growths or *crus bourgeois*.

Cabernet Sauvignon is the dominant grape variety in the Médoc and Graves, although a bit of Cabernet Franc and the softening Merlot is usually planted in most vineyards too. The wines are left for up to two weeks in contact with the grapeskins during and after fermentation which means that lots of colouring matter and tannins are extracted from them. This, combined with the fact that all top quality claret is matured in small oak barrels, means that the wines are very dense and tough when young. The best can live for a century and most classed-growth claret from a good vintage needs 10 years before the tannins have softened to allow the fruit to appear and make the wine drinkable. However, an increasing proportion of less expensive claret is now being made to be drunk young and everyday claret can be some of the most reliable and appetizing drinking available to the wine lover.

On the right bank of the Gironde are two more famous red wine areas, St Emilion and Pomerol. Merlot is the most important grape variety in both of them and the wines produced here are therefore much softer, fruitier and earlier maturing than those of Médoc and Graves. Even the areas themselves look quite different. While the left bank is, in general, flat and unremarkable gravel enlivened only by some rather smart nineteenth-century châteaux, the right bank is rolling wooded country dotted with little farms, almost all of them producing wine. St Emilion has its own classification system, drawn up in 1955, which designates 11 *premiers grands crus classés* and scores of less exciting properties which are still allowed to call themselves *grands crus classés*.

St Emilion wines taste a little richer than most clarets, while Pomerols are even richer and plummier. Pomerol can taste a little like a very luxurious fruit cake, and of no property is this more true than of Pomerol's most famous

Château, Pétrus. This is usually billed as the most expensive red wine in the world and can easily cost more than £100 a bottle for a vintage that is ready to drink. This is not unrelated to the fact that the vineyard, typically for the right bank, is tiny and supply is strictly limited.

Bourg, Blaye and Fronsac produce large quantities of perfectly respectable red wine on the right bank, while Entre-Deux-Mers (meaning 'between two seas', in fact not seas at all, but the rivers Dordogne and Garonne) is a source of much of the red wine labelled simply Bordeaux.

Many wine drinkers fail to realize how important white wine is to the Bordeaux region. Huge quantities of basic dry white are made, usually of the Sauvignon Blanc grape variety with a bit of Sémillon blended in to make it less sharp and searing. The best dry white wines of Bordeaux, some of which can develop great complexity with age, come from Graves, though a wine labelled Graves Supérieures is usually sweet. Entre-Deux-Mers is a great source of dry white wine. White Bordeaux is usually dry if bottled in green glass and sweet if bottled in a clear glass version of the high-shouldered Bordeaux shape.

Bordeaux's most famous white wines come from the Sauternes region. The best of these, almost oil-rich wines, are made by encouraging a curious fungus, *Botrytis cinerea* or 'noble rot', to attack the grapes and concentrate their richness. The pickers may have to go through the vineyard several times to pick the grapes only when they are at optimum ripeness. Sémillon is the most suitable grape, though some Sauvignon Blanc is often blended to give it tang and perfume.

Barsac is a parish, or *commune*, inside the Sauternes area producing slightly lighter wines. All Barsac can be called Sauternes, therefore, but by no means all of Sauternes is Barsac. The most famous, and most expensive, Sauternes is

Château d'Yquem which has earned the accolade of being considered the most highly esteemed gift in Japan. The Premières Côtes de Bordeaux, Ste Croix du Mont and Loupiac areas produce much more moderately priced sweet white Bordeaux.

BURGUNDY

Burgundy claims, like Bordeaux, to produce the greatest red wines in the world, but they are much more elusive.

The Pinot Noir grape from which all good Burgundy is made is notoriously fickle. In stark contrast to the Cabernet Sauvignon of Bordeaux, it has so far refused to travel gracefully and only a handful of bottles made from Pinot Noir grown outside Burgundy can even hint at the delicacy-with-richness that is the hallmark of great red Burgundy.

The heartland of the Burgundy region is a surprisingly thin strip of vineyards, sloping sunwards down from Dijon

Meursault, at the southern end of the Côte de Beaune, is world-famous for its rich white burgundies.

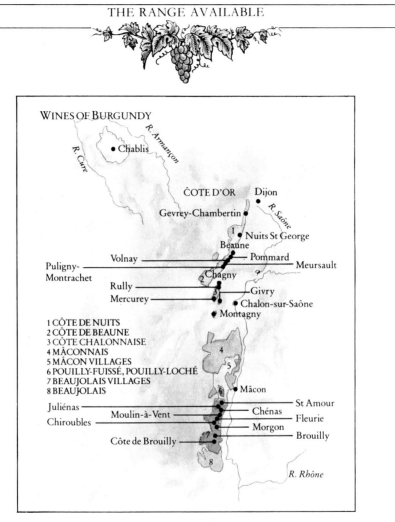

WINES OF BURGUNDY

R. Armançon
R. Cure
● Chablis

CÔTE D'OR   Dijon
Gevrey-Chambertin ●
R. Saône
1 ● Nuits St George
Beaune
Volnay ──── ● ──── Pommard
Puligny-   Meursault
Montrachet   Chagny
Rully ────   2
Mercurey ────   3   Givry
                ● Montagny   Chalon-sur-Saône

1 CÔTE DE NUITS
2 CÔTE DE BEAUNE
3 CÔTE CHALONNAISE
4 MÂCONNAIS
5 MÂCON VILLAGES
6 POUILLY-FUISSÉ, POUILLY-LOCHÉ
7 BEAUJOLAIS VILLAGES
8 BEAUJOLAIS
                              4
                              5
                         6   ● Mâcon
Juliénas ────   ──── St Amour
          Moulin-à-Vent ──── Chénas
Chiroubles ────   ──── Fleurie
                              Morgon
          Côte de Brouilly ──── 7   ──── Brouilly
                         8
                              R. Rhône

to Chagny, called the Côte d'Or, or 'golden hillside'. The
northern half, centred on the town of Nuits-St-Georges, is
known as the Côte de Nuits and produces predominantly red
wines that are firmer and in general longer-lived than the
elegant wines made on the southern Côte, named after the
wine centre of Beaune.

The quality and style of reds in Burgundy somehow varies even more than in the much larger Bordeaux region. This is partly because there is no clearly defined classification system as there is for the wines of Bordeaux.

Most Burgundy vineyards are owned by many different growers who may cultivate only a row or two of vines. Some of these growers will sell their grapes to the wine shippers, or *négociants*, of Nuits and Beaune. These *négociants* will make wine from them and probably blend it with other growers'

The Côte d'Or is the heartland of Burgundy where all the great names are clustered together along a single road.

wines from the same vineyard. Some of the growers will make the wine themselves and then sell it to *négociants*, and some of them will make and eventually bottle the wines themselves to be sold under their own, 'domaine-bottled' label. The *négociants* themselves vary from ultra quality-conscious down to, occasionally, downright unscrupulous, while some of the growers can make wonderful wine and others are simply not equipped to make the best of their grapes.

It is not difficult to see, therefore, that there are few yardsticks on the Côte d'Or. The *négociants* usually try to stick to a house style, which means that one house's Volnay can be much more like their Pommard than like a Volnay from another source. A good red Burgundy will have a cherry-red colour, usually paler than a claret, and a certain sweetness. The bouquet of a young wine usually conjures up thoughts of fruits and flowers such as raspberries and violets, while there are tasters who find mature Burgundy distinctly animal in flavour!

The appellation system is as complicated as one would expect of this region but, in general, the (potentially) finest wines of the Côte d'Or are labelled Grand Cru with Premier Cru representing the rank just below.

If the Côte de Nuits is most famous for great red wines such as Chambertin and the grandiosely priced output of the Domaine de la Romanée Conti, the Côte de Beaune is particularly famous for great white Burgundy, of which Montrachet is the best known. Chardonnay is the grape from which all great white Burgundy is made. Although it has been transplanted to places such as California and Australia much more successfully than Pinot Noir, it is still at its most majestically steely and long-lived on the Côte d'Or. Meursault is slightly more buttery than Montrachet, while the Côte de Nuits' best white is Corton Charlemagne.

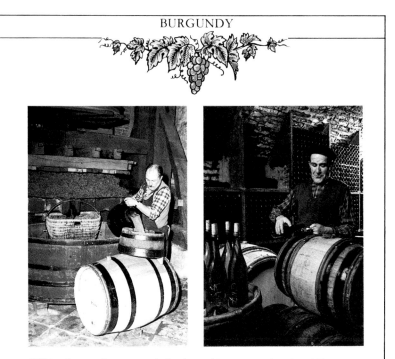

White burgundy is one of the few white wines that is still put into oak barrels. Very good wines can take new oak, while old oak is better for less concentrated vintages.

White wines are given almost red wine treatment by top producers on the Côte d'Or and great wines will usually have been matured, and sometimes fermented, in small oak barrels. The Chardonnay grape is much more dependable from vintage to vintage than the Pinot Noir, though the poor quality of some clones of Pinot planted in recent years may account for some of the vagaries of red Burgundy.

Chablis is the Chardonnay's other great home, though the wines of this northern outpost of Burgundy are usually notably higher in acidity and less opulent, as one would expect of the harsher climate. Oak is now rarely seen in the tiny village of Chablis.

Good-value red and white wines are now made on the

Côte Chalonnaise, as the vineyards round Chalon are called. Montagny is particularly good for whites, while Mercurey reds can be deliciously supple even when young. Rully reds and whites can offer interest at a reasonable price.

Beaujolais and the Mâconnais at the southern end of Burgundy tend to be grouped together for here the Gamay supplants Pinot as the red grape variety. Because of this, Mâcon Rouge is rarely very exciting, though Mâcon Blanc, made of Chardonnay, can often be very good, if not designed for as long a life as Côte d'Or whites. Anything with Mâcon or Pouilly on the label (other than the Loire wine of Pouilly-Fumé) is made here, as is St Véran and the similar, but more elusive, Beaujolais Blanc.

Beaujolais is red-wine country however, where the Gamay grape is at its most exciting. Ordinary Beaujolais and the slightly superior Beaujolais-Villages is a juicy, intensely fruity wine with marked acidity that is designed to be drunk young. Beaujolais Nouveau or Primeur, the wine of the most recent vintage, released just a few weeks afterwards on 15 November, is designed to be drunk even younger. Beaujolais is one of the few red wines that can take this treatment, because it is usually low in harsh tannins and light in body. This means that it can almost be treated as a white wine, and is delicious served slightly chilled.

The most 'serious' Beaujolais comes from nine communes called the 'crus', marked on the map below. Each has its own character, with Moulin-à-Vent being the longest-lived, but any of these can be kept for two or three years to develop more interest than is usual in a Beaujolais. Curiously, the word Beaujolais is rarely to be found on the labels of cru Beaujolais – presumably because the locals are so proud of their *commune*, they imagine everyone else should be familiar with the name too.

RHÔNE

The impressive river Rhône links two very distinct wine regions: the northern Rhône with its statuesque Hermitage and rarefied whites, and the much more extensive southern Rhône, the source of robust Châteauneuf-du-Pape and so much good-value Côtes-du-Rhône.

Those who have hurtled down the French autoroute towards the Mediterranean will know how narrow the Rhône Valley is between the industrial suburbs of Lyons and the gentler countryside around Valence. It takes eagle eyes to

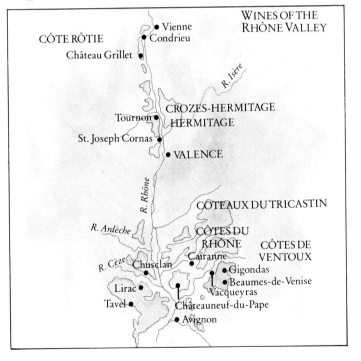

WINES OF THE RHÔNE VALLEY

CÔTE RÔTIE
• Vienne
• Condrieu
Château Grillet •

R. Isère

CROZES-HERMITAGE
Tournon •
HERMITAGE
St. Joseph Cornas •
• VALENCE

R. Rhône

CÔTEAUX DU TRICASTIN

R. Ardèche
CÔTES DU RHÔNE
CÔTES DE VENTOUX
Cairanne •
R. Cèze Chusclan •
• Gigondas
Lirac •
• Beaumes-de-Venise
Tavel •
Vacqueyras
Châteauneuf-du-Pape
• Avignon

spot the vines that are left on the right bank of the river just south of Vienne that constitute red wine appellation Côte Rôtie and the whites of Condrieu and Château-Grillet.

The vines planted on these hazardously steep slopes, Viognier for white and Syrah for red, produce hardly enough to keep a vigneron afloat and it is only world-wide demand for these rarities that makes them a viable proposition. Côte Rôtie means 'roasted slope' and, thanks to a bend in the river, the hillside does indeed face south to the ripening sun. Some producers add a little Viognier to the Syrah for Côte Rôtie, which may then have a special perfume overlying the dense, long-lived characteristics normally associated with Syrah.

Château-Grillet has the distinction of being the smallest appellation in France – a single property – and shares with Condrieu the exciting combination of lots of body and the haunting Viognier aroma that reminds some of may blossom.

Hermitage, the northern Rhône's most revered red, is deep-coloured, dry and lasts for decades. All major north Rhône reds are made from Syrah, though Crozes-Hermitage from the lower slopes around the famous Hermitage hillock tends to be more approachable than most, and to mature after only two or three years. Cornas and St-Joseph are other northern reds and there are now up-and-coming vineyards in their hinterland in the *département* of the Ardèche.

The southern Rhône is France's most sheltered wine region, and some of the reds prove it. Some of the ancient Châteauneuf-du-Pape vineyards around Avignon are especially picturesque, with their distinctive large stones to conserve and radiate heat. As a result, the wines themselves almost taste warm. There is richness and more than a suggestion of the herbs of Provence in most of them.

Côtes-du-Rhône is the country cousin of Châteauneuf, being made from the same mix of grape varieties, in which Grenache and, increasingly, Syrah play a major role for reds.

The Hermitage is dominated by just a handful of producers.

There are white Châteauneufs and Côtes-du-Rhônes, again made from a blend of grape varieties, but this corner is too hot to produce whites with much crispness. Red Côtes-du-Rhône tends to have a certain peppery flavour and can vary between being as full-bodied as a Châteauneuf and being light and juicy like a Beaujolais. Whatever the weight, Côtes-du-Rhône provides good, straightforward, early-maturing wines. Some of the villages in the Côtes-du-Rhône region are allowed to boast their own name on the label. Gigondas is the most like Châteauneuf, while Vacqueyras, Cairanne, Chusclan and Beaumes-de-Venise (more famous for its grapey sweet wine) are all perfectly respectable. Coteaux du Tricastin, Côtes du Vivarais, Côtes du Ventoux and Côtes du Lubéron are the fringe areas of this region. On the right bank of the river Rhône, opposite Avignon, is rosé country. Tavel and Lirac make pink Grenache-based wines that are high in alcohol because they are made so far south.

LOIRE

If the Rhône is red wine country, France's other great river, the Loire, is most famous for its whites. The vineyards along this pretty river are at the northern limit of vine cultivation for France, which means they have to struggle for sufficient sunshine and are almost always notably high in acidity.

For many wine drinkers, both British and French, Muscadet is the epitome of a wine that is appetizingly dry and nerve-tinglingly crisp. It is made from a local grape called

The Loire Valley is intensely, and intensively, agricultural.

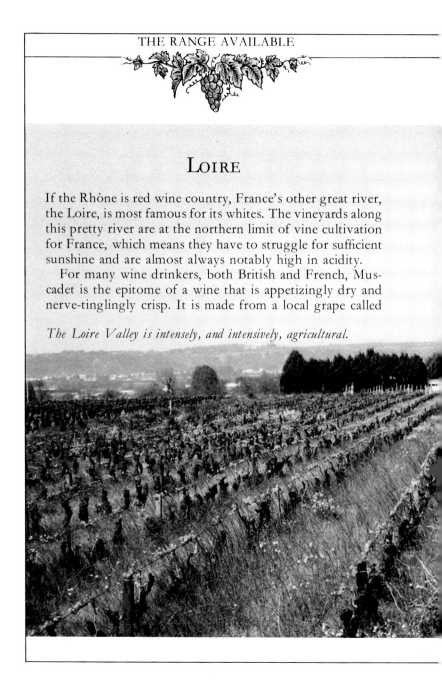

Muscadet in vineyards near the mouth of the river, some of which are also planted with the even tarter Gros Plant. The heartland of the Muscadet area is Muscadet de Sèvre-et-Maine, and the wines labelled *sur lie* are bottled straight off the lees (sediment) to give them more flavour.

Further inland is the Anjou area, most famous for the medium dry to medium sweet Anjou Rosé. Slightly drier and finer is Cabernet d'Anjou Rosé, made from Cabernet grapes.

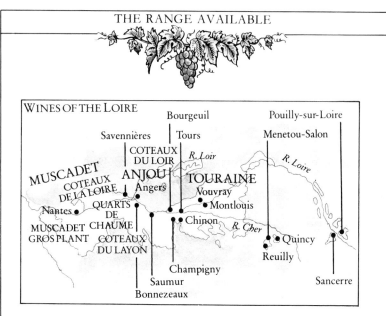

WINES OF THE LOIRE

The white-wine grape planted in the vineyards of both Anjou and Touraine is Chenin Blanc. It produces wines of all degrees of sweetness, but with a slightly honeyed smell, and lots of refreshing acidity. Anjou Blanc is usually a flowery, medium-dry wine, but it's easy to see that it aspires to be a Savennières. This delicate but long-lived prototype of medium dry Anjou white is made in tiny quantities on the north bank just opposite the much richer wines of Bonnezeaux and Quarts de Chaume, the best sites of the Coteaux du Layon. These are French wines that should appeal to lovers of German wine's combination of sweet fragrance and acidity.

Between Angers and Tours is a little red-wine enclave, planted with Cabernet Franc to produce the light, zesty wines of Saumur-Champigny, Chinon and Bourgueil – in ascending order of richness.

Vouvray and Montlouis are responsible for more Chenin Blanc wines of varying sweetness, though the range of quality available as the former is instructive. As with most other wines, the more you pay, the better you get, though no

Vouvray should be expensive. The best, especially the slightly sweeter ones labelled either Demi Sec or Moelleux, can develop a lovely golden colour and intriguing richness over several decades.

The furthest inland of the Loire vineyards are planted with quite a different white grape variety, the crisp aromatic Sauvignon Blanc. Sancerre and Pouilly-Fumé are the most famous products of this area, though the much smaller appellations of Menetou-Salon, Quincy and Reuilly all provide wines of similar zip and fashionable appeal. The tasting term, 'flinty', seems tailor-made for the fresh, yet slightly heady aroma of a young Pouilly-Fumé. These are wines to be drunk when still young and racy. Some red and pink Sancerre is also from the scented Pinot Noir grape of Burgundy.

THE REST OF FRANCE

The *vin rouge* in the French supermarket comes from France's biggest, if least publicized, wine region: the Languedoc-Roussillon, or the Midi. This great sweep of land in the hinterland of the Mediterranean coast is still largely planted with vines suited to quantity rather than quality wine production. Yields of 160 hectolitres per hectare, as opposed to legal maximum limits of around 40 in Bordeaux, are far from uncommon. However, more and more vineyards in the Midi are being planted with nobler grape varieties such as Cabernet or Syrah, and *vins de pays* are usually several cuts above straight *vin de table* from this region.

The far south-west of France has always stamped a strong regional identity on its wines, most of them made from local grape varieties rarely found elsewhere. The viscous white Jurançon, pink Irouleguy, strong red Madiran and red and

white Tursan come from the foothills of the Pyrenees, while inexpensive and accommodating Gaillac comes from the other side of the Armagnac vineyards.

To the north, and all around Bordeaux, are appellations such as Bergerac, Côtes de Duras, Côtes du Marmandais, Monbazillac (for sweet wines), Montravel (dry white) and Côtes de Buzet (red) which provide inexpensive wines that are better or worse attempts at the Bordeaux models. Cahors has the strongest claim for its own identity in hunky reds that can live for years.

In the south-east great progress is being made in the vineyards of Provence. Best known for light, dry rosés, there is increasing and successful experimentation with varieties such as Cabernet Sauvignon.

On the eastern borders, Savoy and Jura are witness to the versatility of French wine, though they are rarely exported. Much easier to find are the delightful wines of Alsace, made from Germanic grape varieties in a dry French style. Such wines are easy to spot, named after the grape from which they were made. The Riesling with its racy fragrance is most esteemed by the winemakers of Alsace, though their customers may know them best by the distinctive Gewürztraminer with its exotic, rich perfume. Pinot Gris, or Tokay d'Alsace, is the third of the three noblest Alsace grapes and makes smoky dry wines not unlike white Burgundy when fully mature. There are some pretty Muscats too, with the unusual combination of grapey aroma and dry flavour, that are traditionally served as an aperitif. The useful workaday grapes of Alsace are Sylvaner and the rather less acidic Pinot Blanc. They may be blended together or with some Chasselas to make a blend called Edelzwicker or 'noble mixture' in Alsace.

All over the country are pockets of vineyards such as those producing the good-value varietals of Haut Poitou, the dry

Château Monbazillac near Bergerac gives its name to a good-value, earthy alternative to Sauternes.

white Sauvignon de St Bris and St Pourçain-sur-Sioule, light red Irancy, the new wines of the Auvergne, and the not-so-little tracts of vines producing Champagne and Cognac.

GERMANY

German wines currently enjoy tremendous popularity, doubtless because they are so attractive to new wine drinkers. Typically, they are white, refreshingly crisp, fruitily flavoured, with a flowery scent, and low in alcohol. This makes them ideal as aperitifs, or even as easy substitutes for water or fruit juice with food.

The Germans are great technicians, and they have perfected the art (or is it the science?) of making clean, scented,

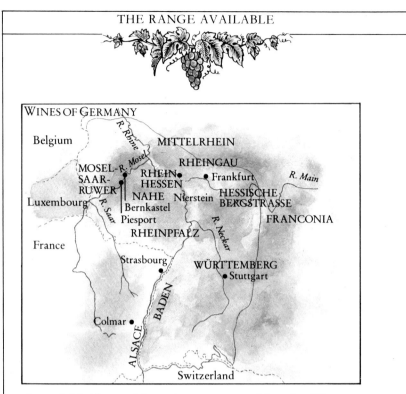

WINES OF GERMANY

Belgium

R. Rhine

MITTELRHEIN

MOSEL- *R. Mosel*

RHEINGAU

SAAR-
RUWER

RHEIN-
HESSEN

• Frankfurt

R. Main

Luxembourg

NAHE Nierstein

HESSISCHE
BERGSTRASSE

R. Saar

Bernkastel

Piesport

FRANCONIA

RHEINPFALZ

R. Neckar

France

Strasbourg

WÜRTTEMBERG

• Stuttgart

BADEN

Colmar •

ALSACE

Switzerland

dependable if unexciting wine at a reasonable price. They are even able to produce such wines from raw materials other than their own. Hence the new 'EEC blends', Germanic white wines made largely from imported Italian wine.

As outlined on page 29, German wine labels may look complicated, but the complications are strictly logical, starting with the green glass for Mosel and brown glass for Rhine wine, or 'hock', convention. Tafelwein is the most basic quality level, often described as Deutscher, meaning German. Landwein is a small category just above this but the vast majority of German wine falls into the catch-all category *Qualitätswein bestimmter Anbaugebeite*, or 'quality wine from a specified region'.

These are the German wine regions most often represented outside Germany:

MOSEL Also known as Mosel-Saar-Ruwer, it includes the names of two tributaries of the Mosel which produce particularly light wines with piercing flavour. All wines from the Mosel, or Moselle as we often call it, are very low in alcohol, often only 8%, delicate in body and very high in acidity. Piesport and Bernkastel are the two most famous wine villages on this beautiful winding river, whose steep slaty slopes are planted with mainly Riesling vines often at a dizzy angle, designed to make the most of the sun's rays.

RHEINGAU The vineyards planted on the south-facing north bank of the workmanlike river Rhine are probably the most revered in Germany. They produce the most expensive hocks, from villages such as Johannisberg, Winkel, Oestrich, Erbach, Eltville and Hochheim. Such wines are in great demand in Germany and are slightly more honeyed than their counterparts from the Mosel valley; their raciness can keep them going for decades.

RHEINHESSEN Hocks from this more southerly, warmer region are softer and less powerfully flavoured than Rheingau wines. This is the region most famous for Liebfraumilch, a blend of medium-dry German wine designed for early drinking, though considerable quantities are also made in Rheinpfalz (see below). Bereich Nierstein and Niersteiner Gutes Domtal are other often-encountered exports from the Rheinhessen. (Nierstein is a commune, Bereich means 'district' and Gutes Domtal is the name of a large collection of vineyards near Nierstein which are allowed to sell their wine, often blended together, as Niersteiner Gutes Domtal.)

RHEINPFALZ Wines from this warm region are characterized by richness, spiciness and much more body than other German wines.

Germany's other wine regions, more rarely represented abroad, are Ahr, Mittelrhein, Nahe, Hessische Bergstrasse, Baden and Franconia (whose wines are very distinctively

bottled in flat green flasks).

In Germany, where sunshine is at a premium, it is the ripest grapes that are most revered – in contrast to hot wine regions such as California and much of Australia where acidity in grapes is at a premium, and the trick is to pick sufficiently early. The most exciting German wines are those that are high in natural sugar and the system for grading superior quality wines rests principally on exact sugar levels in the grapes that went into them.

Qualitätswein, or QbA, wines usually derive what sweetness they have from added unfermented grape juice, called Sussreserve. The top drawer wines, *Qualitätswein mit Prädikat*, or QmP, are sweet because the grapes were very sweet and, even after fermentation, some sweetness remains. The driest of these is Kabinett, then come Spätlese and Auslese which are usually medium dry to medium sweet (though with enough acidity to stop them being cloying) and, richest of all, Beerenauslese and Trockenbeerenauslese (which in the USA is abbreviated to TBA).

This exciting ladder of riches represents the finest achievements of Germany's vineyards. In most years only about 20 per cent of the vintage is ripe enough to warrant QmP status, but the very hot summers of 1975 and 1976, for instance, yielded crops of which 50 per cent and 82 per cent respectively were QmP wines.

Because they are the rarest, Beerenauslese and, even sweeter, Trockenbeerenauslese wines are the most expensive, but the much more affordable Spätlese and Auslese qualities are perhaps more useful. The sweet wines are very sweet, while being delicate too, so they tend to be overwhelmed by food, while being too sweet to be served as aperitifs. However, Kabinett, Spätlese or even a mature slightly sweeter Auslese can make a delicious pre-dinner drink.

The Rhine is as inextricably linked with wine as it is with music and romantic ruined castles.

Riesling (pronounced 'Reece-ling') is the classic grape variety on which almost all other German vines are based. The hardworking grape breeders of that country have been trying to develop new vine crossings that have the wonderful honey-and-flowers flavour of the Riesling, with higher production and good disease resistance. Müller-Thurgau is a century-old crossing that has some of the fragrance of Riesling but less acidity and is much shorter-lived. It is very productive, however, which is why it is now the most widely planted grape variety in Germany. Only in the Mosel does the Riesling still dominate the vineyards. Elsewhere the rather tart Silvaner (Sylvaner of Alsace), Rülander (Pinot Gris) and three new crossings, Scheurebe, Kerner and Morio Muskat are already popular. In good, ripe years Scheurebe can rival the great Riesling, though in poor years its aroma can be just too reminiscent of cats. The Kerner is similar to the Riesling but a bit less assertive, while the Morio Muskat's overwhelmingly grapey scent can sometimes be almost too forceful.

Some red wine is made in Germany, much of it in the Ahr region and most of it either from Spätburgunder (Pinot Noir) or Portugieser, also commonly grown in Austria. German reds are very pale, often slightly sweet, and rarely exported.

ITALY

Italian wine is probably the most misunderstood in the world. Most of us associate it with basic everyday drinking – the very word *vino* is almost synonymous with 'plonk'. We tend to overlook the great wines of Tuscany and Piedmont, names such as Barolo, Barbaresco and Brunello di Montalcino.

In many vintages, Italy produces more wine than any other

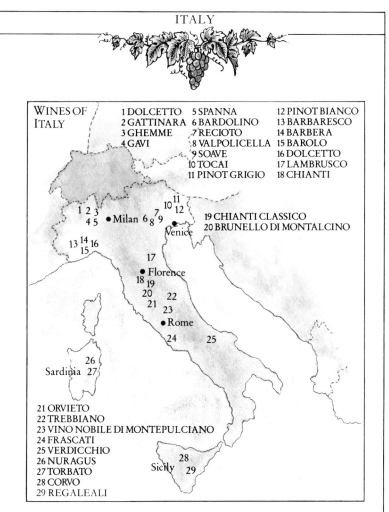

WINES OF ITALY

1 DOLCETTO
2 GATTINARA
3 GHEMME
4 GAVI
5 SPANNA
6 BARDOLINO
7 RECIOTO
8 VALPOLICELLA
9 SOAVE
10 TOCAI
11 PINOT GRIGIO
12 PINOT BIANCO
13 BARBARESCO
14 BARBERA
15 BAROLO
16 DOLCETTO
17 LAMBRUSCO
18 CHIANTI

19 CHIANTI CLASSICO
20 BRUNELLO DI MONTALCINO

21 ORVIETO
22 TREBBIANO
23 VINO NOBILE DI MONTEPULCIANO
24 FRASCATI
25 VERDICCHIO
26 NURAGUS
27 TORBATO
28 CORVO
29 REGALEALI

country. Unlike France, her great wine rival, Italy raises vines all over the country and practically all country-dwellers cultivate a row or two of vines to make wine for their own consumption. Even some commercial vines are still raised among other crops in the tradition they call *coltivazione promiscua* (literally, 'cultivation everywhere'). Because of its latitude, and grape varieties planted, Italy probably has a

better capability to produce fruity table wine, or *vino da tavola*, than its much leaner French counterpart.

The DOC, or *Denominazione di Origine Controllata*, is Italy's slightly unsatisfactory answer to France's *Appellation Controlée* system of designating wine quality. It is true that most of Italy's top wines qualify for the DOC, but some of them do not, for instance, because they are made from grape varieties not allowed under the traditional rules. Furthermore, many distinctly unpromising wine areas have been awarded DOC status simply, one suspects, for reasons of local politics. But then Italy would not be Italy without local politics . . .

The Chianti Classico region is in the heart of Tuscany.

To an even greater extent than France, Italy is above all a collection of regions. Just as their native region is of paramount importance to an Italian, so it is with Italian wines. Because Italy is so far south, her finest wines tend to be produced in the hills, where there is a sufficiently cool climate to prevent the wines becoming flabby, yet they can stay on the vine long enough to absorb lots of interesting trace elements from the soil before they are picked.

Piedmont, up in the Alpine foothills, is the coolest region of Italy, and its wines are the most revered – by those from the region anyway! Barolo and Barbaresco are seen as the king and queen of Piedmontese wine. Both are dark mulberry-coloured, concentrated and exotically scented. These were the first two wines to be considered eligible for Italy's new 'superior quality' category, the DOCG (*Denominazione di Origine Controllata e Garantita*).

Barbaresco is slightly lighter and matures somewhat earlier than Barolo, but both wines are heavyweights to be reckoned with. Impossible to enjoy without food, they are often more than 14% alcohol and develop hints of violet, game, prunes and even truffle when mature. Other Piedmont wines made from the Nebbiolo grape include Carema, Gattinara, Ghemme and the non-DOC Spanna. Piedmont's other famous red-wine grapes, rarely planted outside the region, are the light and fruity Barbera and the dry and grapey Dolcetto.

This is red-wine country, though there is the much-prized dry white Gavi and a huge sparkling wine industry. Its most famous product is Asti Spumante, a sweet, low-alcohol wine that can be deliciously fresh and grapey if well-made, though is sometimes unfairly maligned.

Italy's other major wine region for top quality wine is set on the hills of Tuscany. Vino Nobile di Montepulciano, Brunello di Montalcino and Chianti Classico have each been

The Italians have a deliciously straightforward attitude to wine — as at this family wedding celebration.

nominated for the DOCG, all of them made predominantly from Sangiovese grapes.

Sangiovese is also the most important ingredient in Chianti. It has taken time for this 'serious' wine to shake off its frivolous image. This is partly because some less scrupulous producers have added perhaps too much Trebbiano, the prolific white grape allowed into the blend, so that the wine has lacked colour and body. Well-made Chianti, and almost all of the Chianti Classico that is made in the heartland of the area, is a fruity, scented red that is at its best two to seven years after the vintage. Sangiovese is grown throughout

Central Italy, notably Emilia-Romagna. Sangiovese di Romagna can be good-value basic wine. However, the most successful wine by far of the Emilia-Romagna region is Lambrusco. Low in alcohol and high in fruitiness and fizz, in a sense it is a sort of red Asti Spumante, though less aggressively grapey and sparkling.

One might expect Italian whites to lack acidity, being produced in a fairly hot climate, but this problem is usually avoided by picking early. This may be why Italian whites do not have the complexity of some white wines produced further north, but many of them provide keenly priced easy drinking. Frascati, made near Rome, is one of the most popular and often has quite a lot of body and flavour. Verdicchio (pronounced 'Verdickio') is lighter and produced on the west coast near Ancona, while Orvieto is the most

Domestic vine cultivation in Piedmont in the extreme north-west of Italy.

famous white of the Umbria region just south of Tuscany.

Soave is perhaps Italy's most famous still white wine. The best versions have a distinct hint of almonds overlaying their dry crispness. The red wines made alongside Soave in this Veneto region are no less famous: Valpolicella and Bardolino, the latter slightly lighter than the former, but both designed for youthful drinking and, with their bitter-cherry flavour, pleasant if slightly chilled. The wine curiosity of this region is the *recioto* technique of fermenting dried grapes to produce especially strong wines. A Recioto della Valpolicella Amarone, sometimes known simply as Amarone, can be as much as 16% alcohol and is both bitter ('amaro') and dry.

Up in the far north-east the Friuli-Venezia Giulia region can offer wines most familiar to non-Italian palates. Here an exciting range of 'classic' varietals are produced. Pinot Grigio has been particularly successful among whites, but there has been a great improvement in Chardonnay, Pinot Bianco, Tocai and Rieslings. Merlot, Pinot Nero and both Cabernet Franc and Cabernet Sauvignon vines turn out lively, fruity wines up in this region.

The islands of Sardinia and, especially, Sicily are important wine producers and Sicily boasts a number of concerns that have effectively harnessed technology to compensate for their very hot climate. Among the notable wines of Sardinia are Torbato and Nuragus; of Sicily, Corvo and Regaleali.

SPAIN

Spain's biggest wine export, like that of Portugal, is a fortified wine. Spain's answer to the port of Portugal is sherry, from the baked chalky landscape around Jerez.

Even if Spain's reputation as a producer of lighter wines is not yet established, at least with non-Spaniards, the country

has enormous potential. As the French are only too well aware, Spain has more land under vine than any other country. Much of this land is extremely hot – so hot that it turns out very deep-coloured wines that have lots of alcohol

In parts of the great plain of central Spain, they add white grapes to red wine to make it lighter.

WINES OF SPAIN AND PORTUGAL

and body but not too much refinement. This makes them good for blending and useful ingredients for inexpensive branded blends. Huge quantities of full-bodied wine leave ports like Valencia and Alicante by tanker each day. Valdepeñas is probably the most distinguished of these heady reds, partly because almost all of the grapes used are in fact white, giving the wine made in such a hot region lightness and crispness. It is dyed and flavoured by about 10 per cent of the essence-like local red wine.

Spain's most famous and most respected wine region is Rioja, pronounced 'Ree-ocher' as in the Scottish 'loch'. Up in the hilly wilds of northern Spain it is so cool that the grapes ripen considerably later than in, say, more northerly Bordeaux. In fact, there are strong historical links with Bordeaux

which account for the most distinctive feature of making Rioja: the small oak *barrica* or cask.

Rioja is made from a blend of mainly local grape varieties, notably Tempranillo or Ull de Llebre, grown in one or usually more of the three sub-regions: Rioja Alta, Rioja Alavesa and Rioja Baja. Alta makes the longest-lived wines, Alavesa those with lightness and pronounced acidity, and Baja, usually, the most robust and least refined. Any Rioja that is described as *Crianza* is matured for at least a year in *barricas* made from the richly flavoured American oak that gives the wine a distinctive, warm, 'oaky' vanilla perfume.

The wine is often moved from one cask to another to soften it and stop harsh flavours developing from contact with the lees, which means that Rioja rarely develops any sediment in bottle, and tends to be light in colour. A Rioja labelled *Reserva* is usually at least six years old before being bottled; most of that time will have been spent in *barricas.*

The foregoing comments apply more usually to red wines, Rioja's most important product, but some deliciously rich, oaky whites are also made using exactly the same methods, and nomenclature. The local Viura grape is also the main ingredient in a more modern sort of white Rioja, made without using oak to maximize the fresh fruitiness of a dry white to be drunk young. Some red Rioja being made today exhibits these qualities too but such wines will not usually carry the back label guaranteeing a *Crianza* wine.

Most grapes are grown by smallholders and bought by the wine producers, whose enterprises are usually called *bodegas* – though they rarely look as bucolic as this name suggests.

Navarre just to the north of Rioja makes wines that are similar but slightly less intense, while Penedès in Catalonia is the other major quality wine-producing region. Spaniards have been slow to try out classic non-Spanish grape varieties, but now they are taking to Cabernet, Chardonnay and the

like with enthusiasm. This daring development was pioneered by innovators in Penedès such as Miguel Torres and Jean León. Thanks to their work, Penedès is probably producing a wider range of wines than any other Spanish region. By far the most important individual in this range is the sparkling wine made in San Sadurni de Noya, a little town which turns out some well-made sparkling wine using the same method as champagne.

Spain's most expensive and sought-after wine is Vega Sicilia, from an isolated little pocket of vines grown high up near Valladolid. This rich, spicy red is made from a unique blend of classic Bordeaux grape varieties and local vines which are fermented very slowly and then allowed to mature in small oak barrels, *à la bordelaise*, for up to 10 years, more than five time longer than in Bordeaux.

PORTUGAL

Port, the fortified favourite of the British and French, must be Portugal's most famous export. Her best-known light wine could hardly be more different. Vinho Verde, made just north of the port-producing Douro region, is white, light and, in its natural state, very dry.

Alvarinho (Albariño in Galicia) grapes are hoisted up on pergolas and picked very early when their acidity is still high. This means that the natural sugar, and therefore potential alcohol, is still low, and Vinho Verde rarely has an alcohol level of more than 9%. The wines usually have a just perceptible and very refreshing sparkle, and the exported versions range from bone dry to medium dry.

Portugal's most famous red-wine region is Dão (pronounced 'Dow'), sometimes called Portugal's Rioja. The difference is that Dão wines are usually much fuller-bodied

Many vineyards in Portugal have had to be sculpted out of the hillier parts of the country.

and often considerably tougher when young. They are high in glycerine and tannin and mature versions, up to 15 years old, can still be found at very reasonable prices.

In anticipation of EEC entry, the country has been trying to sort out a system of wine quality designation based on the French *Appellation Contrôlée* system. This is yet to work perfectly, and several of the demarcated zones, such as Colares and Carcavelos produce very little wine nowadays. Bairrada is now making some very good reds, though much of the country's reliable red wine is sold under the name of the producer, such as Serradayres, or called after the principal grape, such as Periquita. *Garrafeira* means special reserve.

A delicious and strongly flavoured dessert wine is made with Muscat grapes grown just south of Lisbon. Moscatel de Setúbal develops a rich golden colour and tastes like a slightly more fiery version of Muscat de Beaumes-de-Venise.

REST OF EUROPE

AUSTRIA As a wine producer, Austria is similar to Germany, but with more sunshine. Many of the wines are from similar Germanic grape varieties but taste slightly richer and spicier. The Schluck brand is a respectable, medium-dry wine made from Austria's grape speciality, the Grüner Veltliner. This nicely sums up the combination of pungency and crispness that characterizes the wines of Austria. Welschriesling is also widely planted.

HUNGARY Hungary's most famous wine is Tokay, a heady golden wine matured almost to a sherry-like state in small barrels called *gonci* and sweetened with hodsful, or *puttonyos*, of *Aszu*, concentrated grape juice. The more *puttonyos*, the sweeter the wine so that a five-*puttonyos* wine is very sweet indeed. Tokay Szamorodni is usually dry, but still quite sherry-like.

The Hungarians, quite understandably, favour their own grape varieties, whose names, and sometimes flavours, are highly individual. The most successful exports are blended reds, such as the robust Bulls Blood of Eger, and Hungary's version of Welschriesling, Pécs Olasz Rizling.

YUGOSLAVIA Welschriesling is known as Laski Rizling in Yugoslavia and is widely grown in Slovenia, notably around Lutomer, to produce inexpensive medium-dry whites. Each of Yugoslavia's six member states has a strong regional identity and this is reflected in the wines. In the south in Macedonia the wines tend to be fiery, alcoholic reds, while some piercingly crisp dry whites are made on the Dalmatian coast. One of the most promising areas, along with Slovenia, is in the cool Fruska Gora mountains of Croatia where the hills rise up towards Transylvania. An interesting range of wines is inspired by varieties such as Sauvignon, Rajinski Rizling (Germany's Riesling), Cabernet and Traminec

(Gewürztraminer).

BULGARIA Bulgaria has set her vinous cap squarely at the western European market, with a great deal of export success. Bulgarians are able to offer extremely inexpensive versions of varieties such as Cabernet Sauvignon and Chardonnay which, if they hardly rival Château Margaux and Montrachet, nevertheless offer very good value. As the vines become more and more established, the quality should improve – provided the producers can resist the commercial temptation to let standards slide. Her own specialities such as the intense red Mavrud deserve attention too.

BRITISH ISLES A surprisingly large amount of wine, of several different sorts, is produced in the relatively in-hospitable climate of the British Isles. Perhaps the least significant in terms of quantity is the wine made from vines grown here, according to the general methods outlined on pages 51–52. In practice this tends to be called English wine, though there are vineyards in the Channel Islands, in Wales and even on the west coast of Ireland as well as in warmer pockets of southern England and East Anglia. Names of wines to note correspond to the grapes – Seyval Blanc, Müller Thurgau and Reichensteiner – from which they are made. Biddenden, Lamberhurst Priory and Wootton are well-known vineyards.

Much more common are bottles labelled 'British' wine, which are made on a large commercial scale from grape concentrate imported from southern Europe and, increas-ingly, Germany. This business was founded on heavyweight dessert-wine styles, but an increasing proportion of British wine is now only about as strong as German wines.

MEDITERRANEAN Wine is produced all round, and even on the shores of, the Mediterranean – although at its southern limit it is already too hot for fine wine. Only the cooler parts of North Africa are suitable for vine cultivation, and any

Moroccan, Algerian or Tunisian red provides heady evidence of how easy it is to ripen grapes here.

The vineyards of Cyprus, tempered by cooling sea breezes, should be able to produce something a little finer. The slightly sparkling Bellapais is a good attempt at keeping freshness in the bottle, but the raisiny Commandaria is probably still Cyprus's most exciting wine. Great quantities of sherry-style wine are also made here.

Much Greek wine is flavoured with pine-resin, and even bottles not labelled Retsina can have a suggestion of this curious aroma, almost reminiscent of the hardware store. Retsina is usually white, while the most popular red brand is the sturdy Demestica. There has been exciting experimentation with French grape varieties recently, notably at Château Carras.

THE UNITED STATES

There is hardly a state in the Union nowadays that does not harbour a vineyard, but commercial wine production is concentrated on the West Coast and in New York State. The Eastern wine industry has been based on native American vines that give a strange animal-like flavour to the wines which can be off-putting to those not reared on them. European vines are increasingly being planted in the East, but even if they take over, the major US wine exporter will probably continue to be California.

Of the many people who have made exciting new plantings of vines in the second half of this century, the Californians have publicized themselves most actively. And, indeed, they have a great deal to be proud of. The 1970s saw investment on a huge scale in planting premium European grape varieties (not always on the ideal site!) and building the best-equipped wineries in the world. All this investment bore

In California's Napa Valley they avoid frost damage by whisking up the cold air with special wind machines.

fruit, and California more than any other region has given the winemakers of France and Germany a jolt by showing such exciting potential for top-quality wine. The 1980s have seen a period of consolidation for the Californian wine industry, by trying to match grape varieties to the right vineyard and by establishing a suitable pricing policy.

The hot San Joaquin Valley supplies most of California's basic wines, often called 'jug wine'. The whites tend to be dependable if unexciting and to be considerably sweeter than French white table wine. All that sunshine can be tasted in some fairly sweet, full basic reds too.

Most of the medium- to top-quality wines are sold as 'varietals', named after the principal grape variety from which they were made. Cabernet Sauvignon has been the most acclaimed of the reds and, given a luxurious upbringing in small oak casks imported from Bordeaux, the wines it produces can easily be confused with fine claret from a very

ripe vintage. The Napa Valley, just an hour's drive to the north of San Francisco, has earned itself a reputation as 'the Médoc of California' on the strength of some of its Cabernets.

So much of California's own special red grape, Zinfandel, is grown that it is most readily associated with everyday blends of varying styles but with a ripe berry flavour in common. However, Zinfandel from old vines can be deliciously concentrated. Attempts with the red Burgundy grape, Pinot Noir, have as yet been much less successful, though there are some excellent Merlots. Petite Sirah is a deep-coloured everyday red unrelated to France's Syrah.

Most of the stunning white wines have been made from Chardonnay, but tend to be much more alcoholic and less steely than their Burgundian counterparts. Sauvignon Blanc has never looked back in terms of popularity since wine-maker Robert Mondavi renamed it Fumé Blanc and reminded all his customers it was the grape of the Pouilly Fumé. The German Riesling is called Johannisberg Riesling here and, although fuller in body, can be quite as excitingly racy and fragrant. Napa's rival, Sonoma County, has produced some stunning whites – and some excellent reds too. Colombard and Chenin Blanc are usually used for medium-dry inexpensive wines.

The Californians have evolved a wine vocabulary all of their own. Wine is made, naturally enough, at a 'winery' and, if it is a small one (and most of the most quality-conscious ones are), it might even be called a 'boutique winery'.

Vineyards are now being planted the full length of the West Coast, as far south as San Diego and right up through Oregon to Washington State. Oregon has the coolest vineyards and shows great promise with Pinot Noir and Chardonnay, while Washington State grows a wide variety of premium varietals in the irrigated Columbia Basin.

SOUTH AMERICA

Grapes are grown throughout the more temperate zones of South America, as far north as the higher reaches of Mexico. Argentina is the fourth largest producer of wine in the world. The reds tend to be robust and taste slightly sweet, and there have been a number of plantings of classic European grape varieties. Chile shows the greatest potential as a top quality wine producer. The vines are not grafted because phylloxera has never struck in Chile and this gives all the wines a noticeably intense fruity flavour. Cabernet has always been Chile's most successful red wine, though there are now interesting experiments with Sauvignon Blanc.

AUSTRALIA

There are strong similarities between the sort of enterprise shown by Australian winemakers and their counterparts in California. Both are extremely innovative, completely unfettered by tradition, and convinced that their best wines are the best in the world. The difference is that the Australians have had a longer unbroken history of wine production, which is today reflected in a sophisticated level of wine connoisseurship. Most of Australia's vineyards are clustered around her underskirts in the cooler, southern limits of the country, though new, even cooler areas are being sought out continuously. It is worth remembering that all of Australia is closer to the equator than Naples.

Australia's common or garden wine, most of it sold in boxes – for they were pioneered here – comes from the intensely hot irrigated river areas well towards the centre of the country. As in California, both reds and whites are characterized by a fair amount of apparent residual sugar, but

Many Australian vineyards are vast, as in the Barossa Valley.

the quality is excellent for the price. Varietal labelling is taking over from the old, and somewhat dubious, practice of naming wine after its European prototype (hence 'Coonawarra Claret' and 'Hunter Valley Burgundy').

Approximately an hour's flight north of Sydney, the Hunter Valley is probably the most famous quality-wine region. It adds its own very particular minerally flavour (sometimes known as 'sweaty saddle') to its most famous red grape, Shiraz, closely related to the Rhône's Syrah. This is Australia's most widely planted grape variety and makes rich, almost chocolaty, spicy wines. Hunter Valley's traditional white grape is Semillon which can mature to golden glory.

An isolated patch of red earth in South Australia called Coonawarra is reckoned to produce the best Australian Cabernets while the Barossa Valley north of Adelaide has a strong tradition in Germanic wines made, increasingly, from the 'real' (Rhine) Riesling. The state of Victoria shows enormous promise with a wide range of different varietals in

recently replanted areas such as the Yarra Valley. Its traditional pride and joy are the luscious dark liqueur Muscats of Rutherglen in the north east. New vineyards in the cool southern tip of Western Australia and Tasmania are currently expected to yield some of Australia's most elegant wines. Chardonnay is currently the most fashionable grape variety, as it is in the USA, and plantings are increasing dramatically throughout the country's vineyards.

SOUTH AFRICA

The South Africans have been making great efforts to improve the quality of their wines. This started with the installation of ultra-modern equipment for fermenting white wines in a hot climate, and is now continuing with a programme of improving the health and productivity of the vines themselves.

Chenin Blanc, often called Steen in South Africa, and tasting much less honeyed than the Chenin Blanc of the Loire, is the most popular white wine. Most whites are left slightly spritzy to make them seem crisper and very few are designed for a long life. There have been some excellent sweet Rhine Rieslings, though Cape or Paarl Riesling is a much less distinguished grape. The South African wine industry, based in the hinterland of Cape Town, has been slow to import cuttings of those two white grapes so fashionable elsewhere, Sauvignon Blanc and Chardonnay.

Cape reds are soft and have a certain warm minerally flavour, though they tend to brown after only a couple of years. Cabernet Sauvignon, as elsewhere, here shows its versatility as a top-quality grape, although Pinotage, supposedly a crossing between Pinot Noir and the Rhône grape Cinsaut, is an ultra-fruity local speciality.

WHAT TO DRINK WHEN

APERITIFS

An aperitif is any drink served before a meal. Ideally, it should fulfil three functions: to refresh; to be easy to drink without food, and to stimulate the appetite.

Many wines make ideal aperitifs, because they offer stimulation in a fairly dilute form. The archetypal aperitif is a glass of dry sherry – a Fino or a Manzanilla. These tangy fortified wines leave the palate razor-sharp and clean as a whistle. Sherry-like wines such as light dry Montilla, Château-Chalon from the Jura or even the dry Tokay Szamorodni from Hungary work on the same principle. They are light wines that will keep their freshness in an opened bottle for perhaps a week. More sturdy are the richer sherries, such as Amontillado or Oloroso, although perfectionists would want to search out a dry version of each. Sercial Madeira is fairly dry, refreshing, and lasts well.

Most fortified wines are designed as aperitifs, although many of them can be too sweet to stimulate the appetite. Dry vermouth with ice and a twist of lemon zest makes an easy and inexpensive start to a meal. Chambéry and Noilly Prat have a more delicate flavour than most. Punt e Mes has an appetizingly herby flavour that you either love or loathe.

The classic, and extremely expensive, aperitif is champagne, Brut or Dry. Bubbles mysteriously add a celebratory ingredient. About half the price of champagne are some very well-made sparkling wines from Saumur, Alsace, Burgundy,

Limoux, northern Spain and northern Italy. Many wine shops sell special stoppers that will keep an opened bottle bubbly overnight.

All sorts of still wines make delicious aperitifs. German wines are usefully low in alcohol and need not be too sweet.

The Muscat of Alsace is a classic aperitif, and most dryish whites can be enjoyed without food.

Any of the drinks listed above would be fine for parties, but wines that are very high in acid can be difficult to digest without the relief of solid matter, so bone dry white wines such as Muscadet seem very tart, and many Sauvignons are not ideal party wines. Any red provided for drinking over a longish period without food should ideally be something fairly light and soft such as Beaujolais or north Italian Cabernet.

FOOD AND WINE

It is sad that people worry so much about matching wine with food, as it really matters so little. The only important aspect is that you enjoy it.

Even the best-known 'rule', which dictates that you must drink red wine with meat and white wine with fish, was made to be broken. Fish tends to be more delicate than meat. White wines tend to be more delicate than red and to have a little bit more of that acid we like with fish, as our taste for lemon juice, tartare sauce and vinegar testifies. Hence a gastronomic tradition that is reverently served up to generation after generation by a line of solemn wine-waiters. In fact some light reds such as youthful wines from Burgundy and the Loire can be lovely lubricants for richer fish dishes. By the same token, white wines such as full-bodied white Burgundies and other Chardonnays can well stand up to meat dishes.

The key element in a wine that determines what food it would taste best with is not colour, but body or alcohol. Robust, strong-flavoured foods need full-bodied wines, while dishes that are delicate in texture or subtle in flavour call for something much lighter bodied. This is simply to

ensure that food is not overwhelmed by being eaten with wine that is too overpowering and vice versa.

For the same reason, it makes sense when serving a sequence of more than one wine at a meal – a habit that indicates a thoughtful host – to serve lighter bodied wines before fuller ones. A dry wine tastes sour after a sweet one, so it makes sense to serve the drier wines first. It is also a good idea if serving wines of different cost and quality, to put the best at the end. Otherwise the lesser bottles will look more puny than they need.

There are a very few foods that are difficult to enjoy with a glass of wine, though highly spiced foods like curries are among them. Globe artichokes and asparagus seem to make wine taste metallic, just as toothpaste does to wine or any other fruit juice. Anything very high in acid, such as a particularly sharp vinaigrette, does little to improve the flavour of a fine wine, though you can always rinse away the vinegar flavour with a mouthful of water or something absorbent and neutral such as bread. A wine served with something sweet needs to be at least as sweet as the dish it is accompanying. Otherwise, all you will taste in the wine will be its acidity. This means that something as rich as chocolate mousse or crème brûlée calls for a really heavy Sauternes or a sweet fortified wine.

DINNER PARTIES

THE FIRST COURSE It is traditional to serve a dry white with the first course as a prelude to a more concentrated red with the main dish; white Burgundy followed by claret is the archetypal, if predictable, pattern. It is fun, and instructive, to serve different wines with each course, but the main thing is that they go well with the food being served. A light Italian red such as a young Chianti or Valpolicella would be lovely

with a plate of salami and other antipasti, for instance. Dry sherry and Madeira are traditional with meat- and fish-based soups and serve as a good reminder that you can always ask your guests to continue with any wines they were drinking as aperitifs, so long as they are not too sweet for the food.

THE MAIN COURSE Almost any dryish wine will probably taste fine with almost anything you plan to serve as a main course. You may feel, however, that you want to serve a wine that will be *just* right as opposed to merely acceptable. Remember to match the weight of the food with the weight of the wine, so that hearty stews are washed down with a fairly robust wine whereas delicate raw ingredients lightly cooked, such as poached fish or white meats, are flattered by a lightweight wine. Take a cue from the geographical origins of the dish. Pasta really does taste good with Italian reds. Red Burgundy seems perfect with coq au vin. Plainish roasts and steaks seem to allow the complexities of claret to speak for themselves. And a goulash would provide a good excuse for the inexpensive Bulls Blood.

CHEESE The French serve cheese before anything sweet, on the principle that it is the ideal foil for any red wine that may be left from the main course. This certainly makes sense if your guests are sufficiently abstemious, although in wine-minded households the cheese can herald the appearance of the grandest wine of the meal. Contrary to popular belief, English cheeses are probably a better accompaniment to wine than many French - particularly the soft ones such as Brie and Camembert that can often get rather strongly ammoniac. Most red wines taste even more delicious with cheese, which seems to soften their rough edges. However, a very salty cheese such as Roquefort or Stilton can take a strong and very sweet wine. Sauternes and port are, respectively, traditional liquid accompaniments.

SWEET THINGS Since any sweet dish emphasizes the acidity

Top quality claret and roast beef make a classic British combination – especially if the wine has been reduced to enrich the gravy.

in any wine, it calls for something that is fairly full-bodied and either as sweet or more so. This means that the light German wines are best enjoyed without food, while Sauternes and rich Muscats, such as the popular one from Beaumes-de-Venise, go splendidly with sweeter foods.

DRINKS AFTER DINNER

The classic spirits offered after a meal are liqueurs and brandies, though connoisseurs are increasingly treating malt whisky as though it too were a brandy. However, there are less heady ways of ending a meal which may gain or regain popularity as breathalysers start to shape drinking habits. Port comes into its own at the end of a meal, and can happily be enjoyed with both cheese and coffee. The different sorts of port available are outlined on pages 60–61 and any of them, except perhaps for white port, would be a suitable after-dinner treat. Vintage port is specifically designed for this.

Bual and Malmsey Madeira would also be delicious at the end of a meal, and their traditional accompaniment of nuts and dried fruits would make an easy and unusual end to an autumn dinner party. Malaga, a dark plumcake of a wine still made in southern Spain, could tackle many puddings head on, as well as providing contemplative sipping long after the pudding plates have been cleared away. Commandaria from Cyprus is even sweeter and more raisiny, though the most exciting blends are as difficult to find as top-quality Marsala, the baked dark dessert wine of Sicily.

The Muscat grape, in its many forms, is a great provider of a wide range of delicious dessert wines that can be served with puddings or after the meal. Sweet, alcoholic and liquorous Muscats are made all over southern France, with those of Beaumes-de-Venise being particularly popular. Portugal's answer is the golden Moscatel de Setúbal, while California has developed a number of sweet Muscat- or Moscato-based wines that are relatively low in alcohol. Most of the newer wine regions have not as yet developed their potential for dessert wines, with the exception of Australia. The liqueur Muscats of north-east Victoria are one of the

world's most under-appreciated treasures, already in danger
of extinction, and would make a delicious if esoteric end to
any meal.

*Port is a versatile drink for the end of the meal, happily
partnering cheese (traditionally Stilton), fruit, nuts and even
some puddings.*

WINE LANGUAGE

Fr – French
G – German
I – Italian
Sp – Spanish

abboccato (I) sweet.

acidity the vital ingredient in wine that gives it life. Lemon juice and vinegar are very high in acid.

aftertaste the sensation left in the mouth after a wine has been swallowed or spat out. An aftertaste could be unpleasant, unlike finish and length (q.v.) which are always signs of distinction.

amabile (I) sweet.

aroma simple smell of a young wine.

astringent harsh, tough sensation felt on the inside of the mouth. Used for white wines when tannin (q.v.) is used for reds.

bead smart term for the stream of bubbles in a sparkling wine.

Bereich (G) large region as in Bereich Bernkastel which is that surrounding the village of Bernkastel.

body roughly, the 'weight' of a wine, closely allied to alcoholic content.

bodega (Sp) building in which wine is made and/or stored.

bone dry very dry, with imperceptible residual sugar (q.v.).

bouquet the developed smell of a mature wine, as opposed to aroma (q.v.).

brut dry to very dry, used especially for sparkling wines.

cave(s) (Fr) premises in which wine is made and/or stored. The term can denote anything from, literally, a cave to a vast modern warehouse.

chai (Fr) Bordeaux term for the premises in which wine is kept in barrels to mature.

chambré (Fr) brought to room temperature.

chambrer (Fr) to bring a wine to room temperature by standing the bottle in a room for three or four hours.

champagne (Fr) only sparkling wines made in the Champagne region by the *méthode champenoise*. All the rest are simply 'sparkling wines'.

chaptalization adding sugar

to the must before
fermentation to make wine
stronger.

château (Fr) the word, with a
particular meaning in
Bordeaux, denotes a wine
property in terms of vineyards
and cellars, and the building
that forms its HQ – even if
no grander than a tiny
farmhouse.

chewy high in tannin and
body.

claret the red wines of the
Bordeaux region.

classico (I) the heartland and
therefore the best bit of a
wine region.

clos (Fr) enclosed vineyard,
often used in Burgundy for a
site with ecclesiastical
connections.

commune (Fr) parish.

cosecha (Sp) vintage year or
harvest.

Coteaux (Fr) higher ground
of a region.

Côte(s) (Fr) higher, superior
ground and appellation. Wine
from Côtes de X is generally
better than simple X.

crisp appetizingly tart.

cru classé (Fr) literally,
'classed growth'. This means
that the property has been
included in one of the official
classifications of the superior
wine producers of a region, of
which the 1855 classification
of Médoc and Graves is the
most famous.

demi sec (Fr) quite sweet,
used especially for sparkling
wines.

dry this infuriatingly inexact
term can cover anything from
bone dry to medium dry
(q.v.).

domaine (Fr) wine property
and/or vineyard holdings,
common in Burgundy.

domaine bottled bottled by
the vine grower rather than
by a shipper.

Erzeugerabfüllung (G) estate
bottled.

estate bottled bottled at the
place where it was made
rather than being shipped in
bulk before bottling.

fermentation the process of
turning the sugar in ripe
grapes into alcohol by the
action of yeast.

finish a wine has a long finish
if its (pleasant) impact in the
mouth lasts for ages after it
has been swallowed or
expectorated. This is a sign of
quality.

flabby one of the classic
examples of wine jargon, used

to describe a wine that lacks acidity.

fortified wines strengthened by the addition of alcohol.

fruit an all-important quality in youthful wine, derived straight from the grape via fermentation.

fruity a wine with lots of fruit.

full-bodied a wine with lots of body.

green unpleasantly high in youthful acidity.

hock any German wine made from one of the regions along the Rhine (as opposed to Mosel).

length a wine has length or is long if it has a good finish.

light the opposite of full-bodied.

magnum a bottle containing 1.5 litres.

medium dry should be between dry and medium sweet, but there is considerable overlap between these terms.

mellow term sometimes used to describe wines, usually red, that are slightly sweet.

millésime (Fr) vintage date.

mis (en bouteille) (Fr) bottled.

mis (en bouteille) à la

propriété/domaine (Fr) estate bottled.

mis (en bouteille) dans nos caves (Fr) usually means the wine was bottled by a bigger commercial enterprise than that which produced it.

moelleux (Fr) sweet.

mousseux (Fr) sparkling. *Mousse* means froth.

négociant (Fr) wine shipper or merchant (as opposed to vine grower).

non vintage or NV a blend of different years' produce, or simply the most recent year available.

nose is used both as a verb as in 'let me nose that claret' and noun as in 'what a wonderful nose that claret has'.

nouveau (Fr) technically speaking, any new wine of the year released after 15 December, as opposed to *primeur* which is the wine, usually Beaujolais, released on 15 November. In practice, the terms are interchangeable.

oaky warm, toasted sort of flavour in a wine that comes from being kept in oak barrels.

reserva (Sp) special reserve wines of a particular vintage.

residual sugar the amount of

sweetness left in a wine after fermentation is complete and the rest of the sugar has been converted into alcohol.

riserva (I) special reserve wines of a particularly good vintage.

secco (I) dry.

seco (Sp) dry.

Sekt (G) sparkling wine made in Germany (though note that only *Deutschersekt* is sparkling German wine!).

soft without very much tannin (q.v.).

spittoon any receptacle at a wine-tasting into which wine is spat lest it intoxicates.

star bright crystal clear.

supérieur (Fr), *superiore* (I) stronger (usually by half a degree) – not necessarily superior. Many bottlers choose not to use the term even when this is allowed.

tannic high in tannin.

tannin an extract from grapeskins and wood which tastes very harsh, like stewed tea, when young but which softens with age to show the fruit in a wine.

varietal a wine named after the grape from which is is produced.

vendemmia (I), *vendimia* (Sp) vintage.

Villages (Fr) selected superior villages of a wine region. X-Villages is generally superior to a wine labelled simply X.

vintage covers both the process of harvesting grapes and the character of the year itself. Thus a vintage can be both fast and poor.

vintage charts little tables rating each vintage for different wine regions should be treated with suspicion as they can give only the most general of pictures. The recommendation of a tried and trusted friend or wine merchant is worth more than a rating number.

INDEX